HILAIRE BELLOC

THE POLITICS OF LIVING

To Oliver
Always loved and always missed.

HILAIRE BELLOC

THE POLITICS OF LIVING

CHRIS HARE

History People UK
sussexhistory.hare@gmail.com
www.historypeople.co.uk

First published in the United Kingdom in 2022 by
History People UK in conjunction with Blacker Limited

British Library Cataloguing in Publication Data

A catalogue record for this book is available from the British Library

ISBN: 978-1-897739-32-7

Design and production: Blacker Design – www.blackerdesign.co.uk

Contents

Cartoon of Belloc by the famous political cartoonist, Low,
kindly gifted to the author by Bill Geddes.

First Word

This book is not a biography of Hilaire Belloc, nor is it an academic evaluation of the man and his work; rather it is a personal appreciation of Hilaire Belloc – warts and all. It may seem odd that I have subtitled this book, 'The Politics of Living,' given that Belloc was a very unsuccessful politician and railed against politicians in general for most of his life. My use is based on the following definition: "A set of activities that are associated with many decisions in groups, or other forms of power relations among individuals, such as the distribution of resources or status." Belloc was very concerned with the loss of status that capitalism imposed on society, for example, the turning of artisans into factory-workers. He was convinced that only the equitable distribution of resources, particularly land, could create conditions whereby status could be restored and a genuinely free society created. His devout, yet fractious relationship with the Catholic church certainly formed a considerable part of Belloc's politics of living, as well as shaping his understanding of, what we may call, the politics of death.

In February 2017, our family was devastated by the loss of our son Oliver to suicide. No one should have to live through such a time as that – the indescribable sense of loss, the pain, the utter confusion, the hopelessness. My wife, Ann, found the courage and the love to create a charity, Olly's Future, in Oliver's memory, to celebrate his life and prevent other young people losing their lives to suicide.

I did not do so well. I somehow managed to cope until after the funeral, and then just went to pieces, and remained in pieces for over two years. Thanks to the love, support and encouragement of family and friends, I slowly put those pieces back together again. My son Samuel and his partner Diana have brought two beautiful children – Magnus and Mabel – into our lives that has brought myself and Ann joy we could not have imagined five years ago.

My gratitude to those people will never dim, but I must also acknowledge the part that Belloc played in my survival: his writings and profound reflections on life and death gave me comfort and helped me keep my head above water when the rains were still falling and the waves still crashing onto the shore. Belloc knew loss. His wife died aged only 43. His son, Louis, was killed in the First World War, and his son, Peter, in the Second World War.

More than that, Belloc was a perpetual outsider – half French and wholly Catholic – he did not fit easily into the Edwardian world of polite society and Anglican values. Like Belloc, I too had a political career that ended in disillusionment; like Belloc I have had a lifelong love of history; like Belloc I have cherished all my life the woods, rivers, valleys and the majestic downs of 'the South Country'. Belloc loved to sing traditional folk songs and so do I. Belloc wrote his own songs in the traditional idiom, and sung them to raise his spirits - as do I.

In this book I have taken themes from Belloc's life and writings that resonate with me and I hope they will strike a chord, too, with readers of this book. Belloc is not to everyone's taste and many today associate him with outdated and reactionary views, including anti-Semitism. I do not stint on discussing this side of Belloc. I do not apologise for him – he would never have wanted anyone to do that.

What I do say is that he has been a good companion to me through the most awful time and for that I will always be truly thankful and, in a spiritual sense, I am in his debt.

Chris Hare, Worthing, October 2022.

More information about Olly's Future, the charity established in memory of Oliver Hare, can be found at www.ollysfuture.org.uk

Light and Shade

THE PERSONALITY OF HILAIRE BELLOC

It is a disgrace and a shame for a man not to want to be what he is, what he has to be.

AELFRIC THE HOMILIST

I hate a fellow whom pride, or cowardice, or laziness drives into a corner, and who does nothing when he is there but sit and growl; let him come out as I do, and bark!

SAMUEL JOHNSON

Sitting in a Parisian café in the late 1920s, the American novelist and hell-raiser Ernest Hemingway was sitting with two literary friends, when their attention was drawn by 'a gaunt man in a black cape' passing them by 'on the side walk.' The English novelist Ford Madox Ford claimed it was Hilaire Belloc, of whom he obviously disapproved, as he had 'cut him dead' earlier the same day. The third companion disagreed: 'Don't be a silly ass,' he exclaimed, 'that's Aleister Crowley, he's supposed to be the wickedest man in the world.'

The story is interesting for two reasons. Firstly it highlights the physical similarities between the two men and also their habit of wearing dark clothing and capes. They were both, by then, in late middle age, and noted for their unorthodox approach to life. Crowley was notorious for his occult activities and alleged Devil-worship. Belloc was known as an outspoken Catholic journalist, and staunch opponent of both capitalism and socialism.

The two men were similar in possessing unbounded energy, both physical and mental. They shared a conviction that what lay beyond this world was far more powerful and significant than any earthly or mortal power. However, in terms of understanding that spiritual realm and how the living should encounter and respond to it, they were polar opposites. We will return to the stark contrasts between these two men in the next chapter.

Making an Impression

Having established that Belloc was both a controversial and, for some, an intimidating character, let us consider the man and his personality in more detail, and start with the impression he left on his contemporaries.

The American novelist Gertrude Atherton met Belloc on his first trip to the United States, when he was only twenty. The penniless young man had made the trip across the Atlantic to woo his future wife, Elodie Hogan. He tramped across America to her home in California, only to find she had entered a convent (more of that later). Atherton was a resident of California and was intrigued to meet this dishevelled, yet vibrant young man, as she recalled many years later:

> He was not an impressive figure in those days. His hair was long and dusty, his hands and linen were never clean, and his clothes looked as if they had been slept in, which no doubt they had .... But he was a 'dynamic personality' and his mind was so blazing that I was always expecting it to explode and burst through his skull. One evening he came to call on me alone, and remained until four in the morning. He sat huddled over the fire, his hands hanging between his knees, his shoulders above his eyes, and talked and talked. Such a flow of words I have never listened to, and every one of them sparkled ... when he turned on that extraordinary mind of his full blast, I could have listened to him for ever. He almost convinced me that he knew more than any statesman in Europe.[1]

Due to this extended American escapade, and the year he chose to spend in the French army, Belloc was two years older than most of the other undergraduates when he went to Balliol College, Oxford in 1893 to study history. He made a great impression on all who met him. That he was half

1   Speaight, Robert, *The Life of Hilaire Belloc* (Hollis and Carter 1957), pp. 60 – 61

French and a Roman Catholic, was, at that time, exotic enough; but his travels in the New World, coupled with his having served in a foreign army – or indeed any army – made him appear somewhat other-worldly to the cloistered offspring of the English public schools, who mainly comprised his undergraduate cohort. Had it not been for the financial help of Catholic friends of his mother's, he would not have gone to Oxford at all.

It was at the Oxford Union that he made his mark. On one occasion, two future cabinet ministers had held the floor, and a restless audience seemed little inclined to listen to the young man with the foreign name, as a student present that evening later recalled:

> As he rose, men started up and began to leave the house; at his first sentence they paused and looked at him – and sat down again. By the end of his third sentence, with a few waves of his powerful hands, and a touch of unconscious magnetism, and conscious strength, the speeches of J.A. Simon and F.E. Smith were as though they had never been.[2]

Another fellow student also remembered that evening clearly:

> His speech astonished, then captivated and dazzled his audience. He spoke with great fluency, without the slightest hesitation and without any blurring of his words … above all there was inspiration and there was movement.[3]

Edward Thomas, the poet and writer of the English countryside, recalled Belloc in his student days. Thomas and a friend were standing quietly on a warm, sunny day at the foot of Boars Hill, when they heard a French song being sung very loudly in "a high tenor voice." It was Belloc at full speed:

> A bicycle swept by, down a steep hill, guided, so far as it was guided at all, by the spirit of the Spring, winged by the south wind, crowned by superb white clouds, and singing that song in a whirl of golden dust. 'That was Belloc,' said my companion, as he lay by the roadside trembling from the shock of that wild career. It was Belloc; and it still is.[4]

2   Speaight *ibid*, quoting Basil Matthews, p. 86
3   Speaight *ibid*, quoting F.Y. Eccles, p. 85
4   Speaight *ibid*, quoting, pp. 82 – 83

This supercharged human being remained restless and emphatic until old age finally dimmed his pulsating energy. Even in his 60s, Belloc could captivate an audience, even a sceptical one. A correspondent from the Chicago Evening Post was caught up in the slipstream of vintage Belloc, delivering a lecture as part of a tour in the 1930s:

> I do not think that Belloc's talents fit him for great public service, nor am I convinced that his convictions lead him in that direction; but no matter. Two full hours of his company convinced me of his genius …. He rose to speak on French fiction. Once or twice he sighted the subject – but a word turned him – and off he went rambling delightfully, talking about his experience as a conscript, his dealings with the French peasant, his adventures everywhere, his ideas, his opinions, his beliefs. And the talk was splendid … it flooded us all, just carried us off our … feet and left us gasping.[5]

The reporter may have been won round, but we are still left in no doubt that Belloc talked about what *he* wanted to talk about, which may not have been exactly what the paying audience had expected to hear.

For more intimate insights into Belloc's personality, we need to turn to those who knew him best – those who wrote biographies and memoirs of him after he died. There is no more vivid a portrait of Belloc than one left us by J.B. Morton, better known to millions as the columnist, 'Beachcomber', in the *Daily Express*. Where others sketch, Morton paints in bright and bold colours and allows us to see the man in both light and shade:

> When Belloc came into a room he changed that room. Even those who did not know him were made aware of a mysterious force which we call personality. He imposed himself by his presence, and without effort. He never in his life made a show of being a celebrity, never attempted to draw attention to himself. The black clothes carelessly worn, the intelligent face, the direct unwavering, penetrating glance of the eyes attracted notice, but the deeper impression one received was of power of energy under command, of dignity, of distinction. He was a many-sided man, but beneath the

5   Speaight *ibid*, p. 189

apparent contradictions and complexities of his character he was all one piece, and easier to understand if you treated him as a simple man. There was in him no trace of hypocrisy or humbug, nor even of affectation. He was a loyal friend and a dangerous enemy.[6]

Morton travelled with Belloc on his many European trips in the interwar years and it was the pace and content of these travels that made the biggest impression on Morton:

> When you travelled abroad with Belloc you had, not one companion, but several; the historian, the poet, the soldier, and the man of wide culture who was passionately interested in architecture, in people, in food and drink …. To get a picture of him on such occasions, one must see a square-shouldered, thick-set figure dressed in black broadcloth, black hat, black tie and stiff collar. He carries a very old portmanteau. His pockets are stuffed with papers. He moves rapidly, with an aggressive half run, half walk, his feet shuffling along the ground. He will be cursing as he goes along, but in the merriest fashion ….[7]

Robert Speaight, Belloc's first biographer, only first met him in 1938, and by the time he met him again in 1942, Belloc's health was already in decline. At that first meeting, Speaight recalled, "Belloc swept in, all sails flying, and talking about the effects of the Reformation in Scandinavia."[8] Many met Belloc for the first time in this fashion!

Dermod MacCarthy sailed with Belloc as a young man, forming one of his impromptu crews of the 1930s. Yet his first recollection of Belloc was from the days of the First World War, when Dermod was a small child. He remembered that his parents had been lent a house at Littlehampton and that Belloc would keep his boat, *The Nona*, harboured there, and also his later vessel, *The Jersey*. At that time, Belloc was at the height of his powers, and editor of the successful weekly paper, *Land and Water.*

6   Morton, J.B., *A Memoir of Hilaire Belloc* (Hollis and Carter 1955), p. 16
7   Morton *ibid*, pp. 97 – 98
8   Speaight *ibid*, p. 1

Mr Belloc's home was at King's Land near Horsham, twenty miles inland, and the harbours of Shoreham and Littlehampton were home ports to him. It was at Littlehampton that he once took my mother sailing in the *Nona*, and running aground some way off the beach, had waded ashore with her in his arms and his coat-tails floating on the water.[9]

This chivalrous and gallant picture contrasts markedly with the first impression Dermod had of Belloc arriving at his parents' house in Littlehampton – an impression of a six-year old boy:

> The news that Mr Belloc was coming seemed to put all the grown-ups into a state of agitation. When was he arriving? Nobody knew. Suddenly he appeared. There were a lot of other men with him. He was dressed in black. He blew in, talked loudly, laughed and then disappeared in the huge car he had come in....Suddenly he was back again. The huge car was outside, the house was again full of men again with their deep voices, laughter and noise, and my father was among them. They crowded into the upstairs room, taking me with them. I was frightened of Mr Belloc and all his followers, and yet they seemed very benign and they were continually laughing about something. I was bewildered.[10]

On the eve of the next war, in May 1939, Belloc was still very much the same man, as he light-heartedly confided in a letter to a friend:

> If my health and temper hold, I shall be in Paris in 20 days hence and babbling away like a shallow brook, chattering away like a flock of starlings, gabbling away like a great Crested Gabbler which is, or ought to be, a sort of bird.[11]

Three years later, old age caught up with him, and held him prisoner for the last eleven years of his life, which we will come to in chapter seven.

---

9 MacCarthy, Dermod, *Sailing with Mr Belloc* (Grafton Books 1986), pp. 23
10 MacCarthy *ibid*, pp. 23 – 24
11 Speaight, Robert (Ed) *Letters From Hilaire Belloc*, letter to Mrs Mervyn Herbert, 1st May 1939, p. 275

The Making of the Man

Belloc's ancestry goes a long way to explain the man. Belloc's father, Louis, died in 1872 at the age of 42, only two years after Hilaire was born. He would have no clear memory of his father, although his mother, Elizabeth 'Bessie' Belloc (née Parkes), lived to be 95, dying in 1925. Within months of his birth, France suffered a humiliating defeat at the hands of Prussia at the Battle of Sedan, communard revolutionaries seized Paris, and the young Hilaire was fatherless. Amidst such calamities, it is not surprising that Madame Belloc decided to return to her native England. Yet even here, misfortune was not far away: a supposed family friend, who had 'invested' Bessie's savings, actually embezzled them.

The young Belloc grew up in Slindon, West Sussex, not because this was an idyllic rural retreat in which to raise a family, but because his mother could not afford to live in London (this was the 1870s and the idea of 'rustic' properties in 'the countryside' being 'select' and 'sought after' was not yet one that had taken hold among the aspiring wealthy). The young Hilaire Belloc grew up with a sense of exile, not just from France, but also from 'polite society' in England. Add to this his mother's conversion to Roman Catholicism, and it is not hard to see how the young boy grew up with a sense of being an outsider.

Bessie's family had a tradition of political activism. Her father, Joseph, was a Birmingham solicitor, manager of the local Liberal Party, and co-founder of the Reform Club. Her great-grandfather was Joseph Priestley, the pioneering scientist and political radical. Bessie herself was an advocate of women's political rights. She knew George Eliot and Elizabeth Barrett Browning, and accompanied Elizabeth Gaskell to Yorkshire when Gaskell was researching the lives of the Brontë sisters.

Belloc was also related on his mother's side to the Swantons – Irish protestants who even had a town named after them – Swantonstown (today known as Ballydehob). His grandfather was a Colonel in the Berwick Brigade and killed an opponent in a duel, which resulted in him fleeing to France where he converted to Catholicism and later became a priest.

One of his French grandfathers was a man of formidable temper who once attacked a cabman who had overcharged him and "beat him insensible." As Belloc later put it, "We have always been a family of guts."[12]

His mother, before fleeing the revolution in Paris, found and tended a dying Irish prostitute she came across in the street and sought out a priest to give her absolution. There was tenderness in the family as well as guts.

We have seen contemporaries describe the focused energy of Belloc, but what was less immediately apparent was the reflective and melancholic side of the man, an aspect of his personality nurtured by the trauma and uncertainty of his early years. Two childhood poems written by Belloc when he was living at Slindon reflect this side of his nature. The earlier, written when he was only seven, was composed in response to the loss of HMS *Eurydice* off the Isle of Wight during a winter storm in 1878. The *Eurydice* was one of the last sail-only vessels in the Royal Navy and sank after a long tour of duty, almost within sight of her journey's end at Portsmouth.

> While it was snowing
> And the wind was blowing
> And the ship was going
> The frigate Eurydice;
> While prayers were being offered from the deck
> On came that cruel cloud to wreck
> The frigate Eurydice;
> Just passing round
> By Ventnor town
> The ship went down
> The frigate Eurydice![13]

Here in a child's verse we have themes that will recur in the writing, both prose and poetry, of the adult: the passing of the old, the journey, and the cruel end. Two years later, still aged only nine, Belloc wrote a verse about the medieval wooden effigy in St. Mary's Church, Slindon, believed to represent Sir Anthony St Ledger, a knight who had fought in the War of the Roses.

12 Speaight, Robert, The *Life of Hilaire Belloc, ibid*, p. 2
13 Speaight *ibid*, p. 12

There is no name upon his grave,
If his grave it haps to be
And his face doth look towards the plain
And towards the calm blue sea.

He lies in a small church aisle,
With a small churchyard in view,
By a little gothic window
And by a shady yew.

He may have been carved for ages
And oft heard the tolling bell,
And he may lay there for ages more
In that church aisle, who can tell?

There is no name upon his grave,
If his grave it haps to be,
And his face doth look towards the plain
And towards the calm blue sea.[14]

This poem reveals a child emotionally engaged with the past and finding solace and peace in doing so. The knight died many years ago and perhaps lived a life of danger and conflict, but now in eternity he looks across a tranquil plain "towards the calm blue sea." All, we feel, will be well.

Belloc would go on to study history at Oxford, and the subject remained for him not a merely academic pursuit, but a window on humanity itself, a means of standing above the hubbub of daily life, to see the bigger picture, as he would later make explicit in one of his essays:

> … for history adds to a man, giving him, as it were, a great memory, but stretched over a longer space than one human life. It makes him, I do not say wise and great, but certainly in communion with wisdom and greatness.[15]

14 This poem is on display in St. Mary's Church, Slindon, next to the effigy of Sir Anthony St. Ledger

15 Hare, Chris, *A History of the Sussex People* (Southern Heritage 1995), quote on inside cover, original source not recorded.

As a young man, Belloc undertook great long walks across England's landscapes, sometimes with friends and sometimes alone. He had already walked across much of the United States, and would later hike across much of Europe, including his celebrated walk to Rome. Speaight highlighted this important trait in his subject's character:

> The impression of physical vigour and intellectual high spirits persists in every reminiscence of Belloc in his Oxford days. He walks with Anthony Henley from Carfax [Oxford] to Marble Arch in 11.5 hours and this record was not broken by the attempt of three undergraduates in 1955. He celebrated [Queen Victoria's] Diamond Jubilee by walking from York to Edinburgh; and he walks by himself from Oxford to Holyhead. He is learning England by physical contact with her contours and her soil. He is probing her history by discovering how she is made.[16]

A man, who in so many ways, was an exile, and was always looking for 'home,' both physical and spiritual, found it in these great long walks and in the discovery and intimacy they afforded him. This was especially true of the Sussex countryside which, even as a boy, he explored and knew, creating within him a deep affinity with his adopted country. As Morton observed: "All that part of Sussex [Slindon and its environs] was the playground of his boyhood and early manhood, and as he talked of it, one realized how strong was his love of England."[17]

Elodie

Yet there was no love greater in Belloc's life nor more enduring, than that for his wife, Elodie. He met the Irish-American Elodie Hogan in London, where she was staying with her mother. As we have seen, he journeyed across America, to seek her hand in marriage, only to find, on arrival in California, that she had entered a convent. On returning to England, he learned that she had left the convent and was not unfavourable to the idea

16 Speaight *ibid*, p. 81
17 Morton, *ibid*,

of marriage; so once more Belloc crossed the sea to America, although this time his mother accompanied him and paid for the crossing and the overland travel.

Hilaire and Elodie were married in California in 1896. Their marriage lasted for 18 years and produced five children. Her early and unexpected death in 1914 was a blow beyond compare, equalled only by the death of his son, Louis, killed in action in the last weeks of the Great War. For the rest of his life – another 39 years – Belloc carried his late wife's rosary beads with him everywhere he went, and once became nearly hysterical in Holborn High Street, when he thought he had lost them. Every night, he would kiss her bedroom door and make the sign of the cross. He never remarried, although he had many female friends, including Lady Juliet Duff, for whom he developed a rather adolescent infatuation. Yet it was to Elodie that he remained constant and true all through the 39 years of his widowhood.

So to know and understand Belloc, we must know and understand something of Elodie. Twenty years after their first meeting, and not long before her own death, Elodie recalled the first impressions that the young Hilaire had made on her, and how the passage of time had confirmed those impressions:

> … considering my complete indifference during those days, indifference and virginal scorn for the whole masculine world, I marvel at my own insight! For I plainly foresaw all his power and realised the greatness of his soul. As he has gone on from year to year achieving and accomplishing, I have never been surprised. It is only my girlish vision of him and faith in him being realised.[18]

The novelist Gertrude Atherton, who had met Belloc on his first visit to California and left us such a vivid impression of the young man, has also left an equally clear portrait of Elodie at that time:

> [she was] a beautiful creature, with hair like polished mahogany, eyes of a dark, rich blue, delicate regular features, and a 'mantling colour.' She had

---

18 Speaight, *ibid*, letter to Father Russell, p. 55

neither figure nor style, and dressed abominably, but with a face like that it little mattered, and she also possessed the twin gifts of personality and charm.

They were indeed a match.

In 1905, Hilaire, Elodie and their young family had moved to Courthill at Slindon. If Belloc had hoped to rekindle the joys of his boyhood and pass on this enthusiasm to Elodie, he was to be disappointed. Although she relished the chance to leave London for the countryside, she didn't warm to Slindon, and even less to their dark, north-facing house. It is a sign of Belloc's devotion to Elodie that he very quickly agreed that they should move somewhere else, and within a year, they had taken up residence at Kings Land in Shipley, the home where Belloc would see out his days, and which, to this day, is still owned by the Belloc family.

It was during the 'dark days' at Courthill, that Elodie took a trip to Paris with her sister. It was her first visit to the land of her husband's birth. In a letter to Frances Chesterton (wife of Belloc's great friend, Gilbert), she detailed her French adventure, and in both her enthusiasm and observations, we sense the wife as the kindred spirit of the husband:

> … So I left Courthill under the regime of Hilairius Primus and came here a fortnight ago. We stayed a joyous week in Paris and we have been here a week. I have still a few days of paradise left me. We saw the Review at Longchamps on July 14 – Eleanor's [her daughter's] birthday. How I wish that you and Gilbert had seen it. It shook my soul, and tell Gilbert that as the horsemen and the guns rushed over the shaken earth I felt like a terrible vision of the Angel Michael the emotion of a magnificent patriotism. My patriotism, by the grace and will of God, has always been the obstinacy of the vanquished, the tragedy of the one who hopes. What a people are these Frogs! Homogeneous, amiable, powerful, joyous, tragic – they are Europe. And always my mind goes back to my Green Island, battered ignominiously; squalid, helpless, waiting and waiting for God to give the word when we may claim St. Michael for our patron. Oh! *when* will the blinded English see what we as a nation would do for them in return for a tardy, grudging,

recriminating Justice! Never, I suppose, as He knows His business best; and, as the Italians say, He does not settle His bills on Saturday night.[19]

Here is the sense of exile, estrangement and the not quite belonging that we find too in Belloc's writings. Here also is the irreverence and wry fatalism shared by both husband and wife.

When Elodie died, part of Belloc died with her, at least the part of him meant for family life and domestic things. In the years that followed, his children were described as becoming rather feral, and although he loved them dearly, he was not really ideal parenting material without the wife that made him whole. Belloc after 1914 is a very changed personality, one tied to duty and to faith. It is not that his humour, enthusiasms and passions disappear but they are forever veiled by grief and pervaded by feelings of loss. Moreover, his appearance changes: at 40 he still seemed youthful, by 50 he appeared old. Someone meeting him during the First World War, when he was in his mid-40s – described meeting 'old Mr Belloc.' He suffered prolonged periods of insomnia matched, at times, with a manic workload. His robust constitution was able to sustain this unhealthy combination until his fires were finally dimmed by a stroke in 1942.

Friends

If family came first, intimate friendships came a close second. Had it not been for these friendships it seems unlikely that Belloc could have faced the battles of the 1920s and '30s with all the fortitude and equanimity that he was actually able to muster. Weary and bloodied from the battle, he could always retreat to the carousing laughter of his friends: the men and women who understood him and accepted him for the man he was. His friendships with women were, in some ways, more absorbing than his friendships with men. It was with women that he corresponded most deeply about spiritual matters, as shall see in chapters two and seven.

Not all his friendships could be sustained. A man who at one moment

19 Speaight, *ibid*, pp. 196 – 197

appeared to speak like a revolutionary, and at another like a reactionary was going to alienate people; as was the man that appeared so dogmatically Catholic while occasion demanded, yet wrote prose and poetry in praise of the 'Holy Moon' and holy rivers and springs. Moreover, a man who held his ground and would not budge. Like Dr Johnson, he was not content to growl in a corner but always came out to bark. Once while driving with Morton, they passed a house where Belloc explained former friends of his lived, but now he was no longer welcome. There were other homes where his welcome had been withdrawn. This he accepted with sadness, as the price he had to pay for his beliefs – beliefs which were far more than opinions – beliefs that for him, were Godly truths.

We should not be surprised that Belloc lost friends. When he was fully roused he was overbearing and, one would imagine, intimidating. H.G. Wells, with whom he had a protracted and increasingly fractious public dispute in the 1920s over the meaning of history, remarked, "talking to Belloc is like trying to break into a hail-storm."[20] Wells was an opponent, but God help you if you were an enemy. By the 1930s, Belloc identified the 'popular press' in England and their proprietors as the main source of corruption and rottenness in the country. He saw them as being mouthpieces of the rich, caring little for truth or genuine information, but acting as propaganda tools. Imagine a public figure today, talking to a pool of reporters from national newspapers in this way:

> Let me warn you, gentlemen, that if any of your masters prints any vulgar sneer about me and beer, they will live to rue it. The men who own the Press in this country were born in the gutter. They are my inferiors intellectually, they are my inferiors socially, they are my inferiors morally. Take it down. Take it down.[21]

We shall come back to Belloc on the attack more fully in the chapter on Politics.

Gilbert G.K. Chesterton was one of Belloc's closest friends, but most

---

20 Morton *ibid*, p. 89
21 Speaight, *ibid*, p. 486

importantly he was the man who thought and believed most closely the things that Belloc believed. Indeed so intertwined were the two men and their opinions, that Bernard Shaw christened them 'The Chesterbelloc,' a fantastical pantomime horse of public life. Yet the two men had very different temperaments, as Morton noted:

> Chesterton was easy going. Belloc was not. It was this difference in their natures which made Chesterton deplore what he called the 'sundering quality' in Belloc's quarrels. When Belloc quarrelled it was no sham fight. It was a battle, and he struck to kill, because, as he said, without battle there is no victory on this earth.[22]

When one of the Oxford dons (professors) pointed out inaccuracies in one of Chesterton's biographies, Belloc was incandescent. He had never forgiven the Oxford dons for failing to give him a fellowship after he graduated, and viewed them as being little better than the owners of the national newspapers, in that their 'Whiggish' interpretation of history existed to justify and exalt the wealthy and powerful who formed the core of the English establishment. Just one verse from 'Lines to a Don' should suffice to show that this was indeed no 'sham fight':

> Remote and ineffectual Don
> That dared attack my Chesterton,
> With that poor weapon, half-impelled,
> Unlearnt, unsteady, hardly held,
> Unworthy for a tilt with men –
> Your quavering and corroded pen;
> Don poor at Bed and worse at Table,
> Done pinched, Don starved, Don miserable;
> Don stuttering, Don with roving eyes,
> Don nervous, Don of crudities;
> Don clerical, Don ordinary,
> Don self-absorbed and solitary;
> Don here and there, Don epileptic;

22 Morton *ibid*, p. 77

Don puffed and empty, Don dyspeptic;
Don middle-class, Don sycophantic,
Don dull, Don brutish, Don pedantic;
Don hypocritical, Don bad,
Don furtive, Don three-quarters mad;
Don (since a man must make an end),
Don that shall never be my friend.[23]

Belloc certainly took no prisoners. He could be very rude and rarely masked his feelings. Morton tells of a man who came up to Belloc at a meeting, and cautiously introduced himself by saying, "you won't remember me" – "oh yes I do!"[24] replied Belloc and walked off.

Yet to think of him as a bully would not be fair. A bully takes pleasures and delight in belittling and humiliating a person he perceives as being intellectually or physically inferior to him. Belloc was not like that, as Morton explains:

> The point I would make is that Belloc dominated not by insensitive loud-ness, but by the force of his character. He talked with authority. If some well-intentioned person with nothing particular to say, but anxious to make a showing, broke into whatever Belloc was talking about, he was listened to with the utmost mildness, and I always noticed that if the remarks were deplorably stupid, there would be no reply. Those who expected to see the unfortunate man crushed or ridiculed were disappointed. Belloc was inca-pable of the hypocrisy of pretending to agree with something he believed to be false, but his sensibility and courtesy forbade him to fight the unarmed.[25]

As we shall see in the next chapter on Religion, Belloc saw truth and sim-plicity as two sides of the same coin, and so it was with people: he mis-trusted those who seemed to overcomplicate their arguments and indulge in concepts and use language that excluded the uninitiated from the con-versation. He valued intelligence and knowledge, but not the theorising and intellectual indulgence.

23 Wilson, A.N., *Hilaire Belloc, Complete Verse* (Pimlico 1991), Lines to a Don, p. 59
24 Morton, *ibid*, p. 18
25 Morton *ibid*, pp. 89 – 90

Morton noted Belloc's friendship with Tommy Pope, a man who had neither intellectual nor physical prowess, but whose soul seemed pure and true:

> Tommy Pope [was] one of those self-effacing, meek men who seem to be helpless in the face of the world. Belloc saw the simplicity of Pope and loved him for it ....They made an odd couple, but their friendship was solid and enduring, and serves as an example of an unexpected facet of Belloc. He was always attracted to goodness, to quiet sincerity and to the uncomplicated.[26]

This 'facet' could also be extended to his political opponents. As we shall see in the chapter on Politics, after 1912 Belloc was an outspoken opponent of state socialism and vehemently denounced the Bolshevik takeover in Russia; but that did not blind him to good people, even if he believed they had chosen a bad path. The utopian socialist, Stephen Reynolds, would be a case in point. Reynolds, who tried to live a socialist life and turn away from his privileged upbringing, died at a young age from the 'Spanish Flu' that ravaged Britain and Europe in the aftermath of the Great War. Writing some years later, Belloc described Reynolds as "that strongest-souled and most sincere of men, who desired and did good all his life."[27]

Belloc's happiness came from his friendships and even in chance meetings with strangers – this was his escape from the relentless battlefield of public life. On one occasion he arranged to meet some friends in an alehouse and although others of his class and learning might have found the clientele vulgar, it rather delighted Belloc:

> In the inn, in the main room of it, I found my companions. A gramophone fitted with a monstrous trumpet roared out American songs, and to this sound the servants of the inn were holding a ball. Chief among them a woman of a dark and vigorous kind danced with amazing vivacity, to the applause of her peers. With all this happiness we mingled.[28]

26 Morton *ibid*, p. 19
27 Belloc, Hilaire, *The Cruise of the Nona* (Constable & Co, 1925), pp. 129–130
28 Speaight, *ibid*, quoting from Belloc's 'The Old Road', p. 187

The man who wrote an epic verse entitled 'Heroic Poem in Praise of Wine,' was always going to value friends who provided him with the very best that the juice of the vine had to offer, as we see in this letter written to Gilbert Moorhead:

> By God you are, a splendid fellow, a man worth of many oxen! I have just concluded sufficient and considerable degustation of your astounding wine on which it is so difficult to write that I hesitate and ferret for words. Glory to God who made this wine! It has the nineteen qualities of general wine and added to these the four requisites of strong wine, the eight fundamentals of old wine and the seven excellences of Port in especially which seven are perhaps found united in no other wines but yours.[29]

Wine was second only to people in his loyalty and affection.

Chesterton was surely remembering his first meeting with Belloc on the South Downs, when he wrote:

> When you came over the top of the world
> On the great day on the Downs,
> The air was crisp and the clouds were curled,
> When you came over the top of the world,
> And under your feet were spire and street
> And seven English towns.
>
> For you came out on the dome of the earth
> Like a vision of victory,
> Out on the great green dome of the earth
> As the great blue dome of the sky for girth,
> And under your feet the shires did meet
> And your eyes went out to sea.
>
> And I thought of a thundering flag unfurled
> And the roar of the burghers' bell:
> Beacons crackled and bolts were hurled
> As you came over the top of the world;

---

29 Speaight, *Letters to Hilaire Belloc, ibid*, p. 63

And under your feet were chance and cheat
And the slime of the slopes of hell.[30]

Lord Stanley, in his tribute to Belloc, summed up all that his friends loved about Belloc, what they treasured and what they would miss:

We loved his prejudices because they were fruitful of such spirited debate. He never really expected his friends to share all his passionately held doctrines. We loved the songs he sang; and above all we loved the tender kindliness and courtesy, the understanding of others' trouble, and the ready sharing of pleasure which was always at the disposal of his friends. We loved him for the beauty he expressed for us and for the assured benediction his presence always brought when reassurance was needed in times of perplexity.[31]

---

30 *The Collected Poems of G.K.Chesteron* (Cecil Palmer 1927), 'On the Downs,' p. 63
31 Belloc, Hilaire, *The Cruise of the Nona* (Constable & Co 1955), introduction by Lord Stanley of Alderney, p. xxix

An Enduring Faith

CATHOLICISM, PAGANISM, AND THE JOURNEY OF THE SOUL

It was necessary that there should be sin; but all shall be well, and all shall be well, and all manner of things shall be well.
JULIAN OF NORWICH

Writing a book about Hilaire Belloc without mentioning his religious faith, would not just be an oversight, it would be absurd – for without his faith he would have been an entirely different person. Without faith, he might have been crushed by bereavement, or corrupted by politics. Without faith, he may have succumbed to the egotistic allure of power and wealth. Yet Belloc's Catholicism was not straight-forward, indeed he often troubled his co-religionists, and today few in the Catholic church would wish to claim him as one of their own. This chapter seeks to unpick the complexities of Belloc's religious and spiritual beliefs. Even when we have untangled the strands as best we can, there is no saying that a few stubborn knots will not remain.

Belloc the Catholic

Of all those who have written about Belloc, none knew him better or perceived him more clearly than J.B. Morton:

> To understand Belloc fully, to get any picture of him in right proportion, it is essential to know from what source he drew his steadfast courage, what is was that made him so persistent and so enthusiastic a champion of unpopular causes, what was the driving force in him, what alone explains

him. His religion, as he said, was not a theory, not a mood, nor a wonderful story. It was Reality, a Thing.[1]

"The Catholic Church," Belloc wrote, "is a thing of which a man never despairs or is ashamed." It might be subject to criticism and the individual believer may suffer from waves of doubt, but the eternal truth of revealed faith will sustain and strengthen him. The Church had to be a permanent and stable presence in a world of flux and change. Christ had conquered the world, its snares and temptations. By this means only, he wrote to a friend, "the world has been saved." It should be understood that "all that great scheme is not mist or a growth, but a thing outside ourselves and time."[2]

It was both the timelessness and the universality of the Catholic Church that convinced Belloc of its truth and also comforted him on his travels; which were rarely undertaken for pleasure, but either to earn or to promote and defend those causes that he held dear. In *The Path to Rome*, that extraordinary trip he took on foot, across Europe, to the holy city, Belloc remarked that wherever he stopped, in town or village, highland or plain, small rustic chapel, or vast solemn cathedral, it was still the same Mass, the same words, the same ritual; just as it had been for nearly two thousand years. This greatly moved him, and even more so when he was a great distance from home, or in those years when age was wearying him.

In 1923, Belloc travelled across the Atlantic to New York, the first time he had visited the United States since his youth. To save money, he travelled on an old boat that had seen better days. It was no ocean-going liner, but small and cramped. The crossing had been advertised as taking nine days, but that did not take into account "the progress of as horrible a storm as I have seen in my life," which almost doubled the journey time. Belloc described "the ceaseless roar of the wind and the thud of the seas" on the side of the boat. Yet, it was the most aged of the passengers who proved the most durable:

---

1   Morton, J.B., *A Memoir of Hilaire Belloc* (Hollis & Carter 1955), p. 130
2   Speaight, Robert, *Letters from Hilaire Belloc* (Hollis & Carter 1958), p. 7, letter to J.S.Philimore

The only French man on board is an excellent old Priest from Provence, a Dominican, with a long white beard. He says Mass every morning at an improvised altar table in [the] lounge, and catches hold of a fixed chair while he says it to keep steady. The Missal part he reads out of a book held in his hand. The Mass said under such difficulties is a great comfort.[3]

Here was faith in practical action: offering succour and comment to a soul in distress. Belloc (as we shall see) had little interest in theological debate or the finer points of the liturgy. It was the simplicity of faith and of worship that most affected him. Not long after arriving in America on the hazardous sea journey just described, he attended Mass. Hearing a choir of children singing "moved me to tears of tenderness for I felt then the Faith to be truly universal."[4]

Belloc the Pagan

So is that not the end of the matter? A Catholic who was happiest worshipping in the manner of a medieval peasant rather than a twentieth-century intellectual? For all Belloc wrote with passion about the 'truth' of the Church, he was never far away from another spiritual landfall, and one that persisted throughout the fifty years or more of his published literary output. Let us start with this passage from *The Path to Rome*, published in 1902, when Belloc was 32. Here he is describing seeing – for the first time – the Alps rising up on the horizon:

Here were these magnificent creatures of God, I mean the Alps, which now for the first time I saw from the height of the Jura; and because they were fifty or sixty miles away, and because they were a mile or two high, they were become something different from us others, and could strike one motionless with the awe of supernatural things. Up there in the sky, to which only clouds belong and birds and the last trembling colours of pure light, they stood fast and hard; not moving as do the things of the sky. They were as distant as the little upper clouds of summer, as fine and tenuous; but in their reflection and

3   Speight, Robert (Ed), *Letters from Hilaire Belloc* (Hollis & Carter), pp. 131 – 132.
4   Speight, *Letters, ibid*, p. 141, letter to Maurice Baring.

in their quality as it were of weapons (like spears and shields of an unknown array) they occupied the sky with sublime invasion: and the things proper to the sky were forgotten by me in their presence as I gazed.[5]

Perhaps we could say that Belloc was imagining the 'heavenly host' as he perceived this ethereal army? Perhaps we could, or perhaps there is something of pagan antiquity in this vision – of Homer, or even of the great sagas of pagan Scandinavia, or the martial tales of Irish mythology – of which he was very familiar. Two paragraphs on, Belloc makes his thoughts and feelings more explicit:

> These, the great Alps, seen thus, link one in some way to one's immortality. Nor is it possible to convey, or even suggest, those few fifty miles, and those few thousand feet; there is something more. Let me put it thus: that from the height of Weissenstein I saw, as it were, my religion. I mean, humility, the fear of death, the terror of height and of distance, the glory of God, the infinite potentiality of reception whence springs that divine thirst of the soul ....[6]

Landscape and its associated holiness is a recurring theme in Belloc's writing, and one we will revisit in the chapter on *The Four Men*. Yet, even more significant than landscape is the imagery and spiritual power of the moon. One of the most memorable passages in *The Four Men* deals directly with the glory and majesty of this heavenly body. In *The Cruise of the Nona*, he describes lying at anchor off Shoreham Harbour one still, moonlit summer's night. Belloc was moved by all he saw and all he felt: "A great full moon rose up out of the east, out of the seas of England and the night was warm. There was a sort of holiness about the air. I was glad that we had thus to lie under such a calm and softly radiant sky, with its few stars paling before their queen."[7]

In her pioneering work on Sussex folklore in 1868, Charlotte Latham

5   Belloc, Hilaire, *The Path to Rome* (Thomas Nelson and Sons 1902), pp. 158 – 159
6   Belloc, *ibid*, p. 159
7   Belloc, Hilaire, *The Cruise of the Nona* (Constable & Co. 1955, originally published, 1925), p. 345

identified the powerful role that the moon played in the life of the country people, which she traced back to their Saxon pagan past. Here was Belloc, adrift off the Sussex coast, still paying homage to this old goddess of long ago. Or was it mere whimsy – a sentimental reaction to a beautiful moment at sea? Yet there is far more than sentiment in Belloc's poem, 'The Moon's Funeral.' It can be read as a rumination on the moon's waxing and waning, but could it also be read as a lament for an old religion, lost, but not entirely forgotten?:

The Moon is dead. I saw her die.
She in a drifting cloud was drest,
She lay along the uncertain west,
A dream to see.
And very low she spake to me:
'I go where none may understand,
I fade into the nameless land,
And there must lie perpetually.'
And therefore loudly, loudly I
And high
And very piteously make cry:
'The Moon is dead. I saw her die.'

And will she never rise again?
The Holy Moon? Oh, never more!
Perhaps along the inhuman shore
Where pale ghosts are
Beyond the low lethean fen
She and some wide infernal star…
To us who loved her never more,
The Moon will never rise again.
Oh! never more in nightly sky
Her eye so high shall peep and pry
To see the great world rolling by.
For why?
The Moon is dead. I saw her die.

The Moon, and we must assume, those that worshipped her, are dispatched to lethe waters, where all dreams of former life will be forgotten. And what of the sun – not mentioned by name – but alluded to as 'some wide infernal star.' Many cultures worshipped the sun, but those living on our cold and wet islands far preferred the moon, and they far preferred night to day. This historic truth either consciously or semi-consciously permeated Belloc's thoughts and writings. Morton recalled a little verse of Belloc's own composition that he would often recite:

> The moon on the one hand, the dawn on the other:
> The moon is my sister, the dawn is my brother,
> The moon on my left and the dawn on my right,
> My brother, good morning: my sister, goodnight.[8]

Note that the sun is not mentioned in this verse either, but sublimated into 'the dawn,' which owes as much to night as it does to day. Either way, it is an interesting 'matins' for a Catholic man.

European Spiritual Home

When the sun was up, Belloc enjoyed nothing so much as to walk by the banks of Sussex rivers and search for springs. An old resident of Shipley in West Sussex, who remembers Belloc living in the village, told this writer that Belloc would ask the man's older brother to go to a local spring and fill bottles of water for him from this special source.[9] It should be assumed that well water in the village was perfectly drinkable, and as this was many years before fluoride was added to tap water, it is hard to believe that Belloc thought that the more accessible water was unsafe to drink; it must be that he believed this spring water had a special and 'holy' quality.

Both the Arun and the Adur that 'rise' near Belloc's home at Shipley and enter the sea at his 'home ports' of Littlehampton and Shoreham

---

8   Morton, *ibid*, p. 41
9   Interview conducted by the author with Bob Philips of Shipley. An edited version of the interview can be found at www.southdownsgenerations.org.uk

respectively, are frequently venerated in Belloc's writings, as were other streams and rivers that brought him 'relief from the affairs of men.' He was once inspired to commend the Western Rother, that flows by Petworth and Midhurst, in glowing terms: "If ever again we have a religion in the South Country, we will have a temple to my darling river. It shall be round, with columns and a wall, and there I will hang a wreath in thanksgiving for having known the river."

So, was Belloc's Catholicism all a fraud, a front of respectability? Being a Catholic in England at the turn of the last century may not have been as difficult as it had been a hundred years earlier, or as dangerous as it had been a century or two before that, but it was hardly respectable. What is more, Belloc had no interest in adopting views and beliefs to fit in with other people; in fact, he was far happier taking the opposite approach. There can be no doubt that his Christianity was sincere and central to who he was; so how do we reconcile Belloc the Catholic with Belloc the pagan?

We should begin with his upbringing and his schooling. As we saw in the first chapter, Belloc's early years were marked by war, revolution, exile from the land of his birth, the defrauding of the family fortune and banishment from respectable London life to a rustic existence in a remote West Sussex village. The only constants in his early life were his mother and the Catholic Church. At the age of ten, Belloc went to board at the Oratory School at Brompton.

In later life, Belloc wrote that the school "taught me to fear none but God and speak the truth and be in everything an English Gentleman," but, he tells us, "it never took." So what did take? Belloc tells us that too:

> As for the Classics all my generation ought to thank God they were well whipped into them – for Latin and Greek are tasks for boys and it is as tasks and discipline that they take root. Then in later life they bear glorious fruit.[10]

Homer, Virgil and Horace were a lifeblood in Belloc's veins and told him all he needed to know about human nature. He constantly references the world of 'pagan antiquity'. He tells the story of his time in the French army

---

10 Speaight, *Life of Hilaire Belloc*, p. 32

when, at the end of a hard day's march, the officer went to inscribe the name of the regiment on a mountain wall, close to where they had rested for the night, but found someone had been there before him. There, clearly visibly, were the words of a Roman officer, of perhaps 2,000 years earlier, who had recorded the victory of the third legion. "The words," Belloc wrote, "stood out to silence him."[11]

On another occasion, Belloc came across an inscription on a long-abandoned tomb, dedicated to "some priestess of Isis," who had died in the woods among the "divinities she served so well." "Twice," Belloc wrote, "I read those delicate words, delicately chiselled in the hard stone and I saw her going in black, with her head bent, through the groves." Latin opened doors for the young Belloc into the world of the ancestors, and brought to life for him not just their history, but their religion too.

Belloc was always conscious of the link between pagan antiquity and his own times, and he believed that it was Christianity, and Christianity alone, that maintained the continuity of civilisation and that this was only possible through the agency of the Catholic Church:

> The Thing that is the core and soul of all our history for fifteen hundred years, and into the present time: the continuator of all our Pagan origins, transformed, baptised, illuminated; the matrix of such culture as we still retain.[12]

In a letter to Chesterton, Belloc concisely set out his world view and his religious view; this was at a time when Chesterton was still considering converting to the Catholic faith:

> I desire you to remember that we are Europe; we are a great people. The faith is not an accident among us, nor an imposition, nor a garment; it is bone of our bone and flesh of our flesh: it is a philosophy made by and making ourselves. We have adorned, explained, enlarged it; we have given it visible form. This is the service we Europeans have done to God. In return he made us Christians.[13]

11 Speaight *ibid*, p. 201
12 Quoted from 'A Cautionary Tales,' Wilson, A.N., in *The Tablet*, 25th July 2020
13 Speaight, *ibid*, p. 390

This is hardly orthodox theology. Belloc is implying, at the very least, that the people of Europe, the civilisation of Europe, has made a compact with God: they are the new chosen people. It is from this deeply-held belief that, in part, his antagonism towards the Jewish religion stemmed and led to accusations of anti-Semitism (which I will address in chapter five); it also led him to regard Islam as a 'great heresy.' Such convictions are anathema to the secular Europe of the 21st Century, although recent election results across the continent suggest that our secular orthodoxy is experiencing a push back from the old. This brings us to Belloc's politics, which we will also consider in chapter four.

It was always simplicity that moved Belloc in matters of spiritual belief. The simple mass. The simple pleasure of seeing the sun set over his beloved hills at dusk. In 1928, he travelled to Poland to visit the shrine of the 'Black Madonna of Częstochowa,' and to marvel at the number of people attending the annual pilgrimage:

> The enormous number of Pilgrims to Chestochowa [sic] was impressive to the boundary of the sensational – and across it. We missed the biggest lot which was [for] the Assumption, when there were 300,000 all there together, camping all round the isolated hill.[14]

The shrine itself greatly impressed him (he brought with him his own poem dedicated to the Black Madonna, which he placed on the shrine). He noted that the pilgrims were peasants and workers, and that it was not a place to which the bourgeois or wealthy came. We can imagine that even the idea of a black Madonna would have been regarded as vulgar, even blasphemous, by much of polite religious society in England; but Belloc rejoiced in it:

> The Pilgrims swarm all over the place, going freely by corridor and halls and cramming, in Mass after Mass, the central shrine with its Holy Picture. They shout hymns. They smell very homely: they are the poor of God. All those who hate the poor will do well to avoid the Shrine and indeed all good things.[15]

14 Speaight, Letters to Hilaire Belloc, *ibid*, pp. 201 – 202
15 Speaight, *ibid*, p. 202

The Theology of Conflict and Injustice

For Belloc, the gathering up of riches was not just a foolish distraction, it was an evil at odds with the tenets of the faith. In this view, he had been greatly influenced in his youth by Cardinal Manning, who had declared that "all conflict is ultimately theological." In 1889, Manning, then aged 81, processed into the East End of London, dressed in all his canonical robes and accompanied by priests and altar-boys, similarly attired, to hold a Mass for the striking dock workers. The strike had been bitter and protracted, and Manning's intervention decisively shifted the outcome in favour of the strikers. He had not endorsed the strike nor commented on the strikers' demands, but his mere presence was enough: his actions spoke louder than any words.

In later life, Belloc recalled his meetings with the cardinal and from his comments we can readily see the powerful influence that the old man had on Belloc:

> It was my custom during my first days in London, as a very young man, before I went to Oxford, to call upon the Cardinal as regularly as he would receive me; and during those brief interviews I heard from him many things which I have had later occasions to test by the experience of human life. I was, it may be said, too young to judge things so deep as sanctity and wisdom; but, on the other hand, youth has vision, especially upon elemental things; and Manning did seem to me (and still seems to me) much the greatest Englishman of his time…. He never admitted the possibility of compromise between Catholic and non-Catholic society. He perceived the necessary conflict and gloried in it.[16]

That last sentence makes for uncomfortable reading to a modern mind accustomed to ideas of equality and diversity and reminds us both of Belloc's intransigence regarding matters of belief and truth and our present-day challenges in deciding what it is we truly believe and at what point we put our 'mark in the sand,' beyond which we will not cross. Belloc

16 Wilson, A.N. Hilaire Belloc (Hamish Hamilton 1985), p. 24

had no doubts where his boundaries lay, nor his response to injustice, as he starkly set out in his poem, 'The Poor of London':

Almighty God, whose justice like a sun
Shall coruscate along the floors of Heaven,
Raising what's low, perfecting what's undone,
Breaking the proud and making odd things even,
The poor of Jesus Christ along the street
In your rain sodden, in your snows unshod,
They have nor hearth, nor sword, nor human meat,
Nor even the bread of men: Almighty God.

The poor of Jesus Christ whom no man hears
Have waited on your vengeance much too long.
Wipe out not tears but blood: our eyes bleed tears.
Come smite our damned sophistries so strong
That thy rude hammer battering this rude wrong
Ring down the abyss of twice ten thousand years.[17]

Navigating the Spiritual Journey

Christ – his divinity, his death, his resurrection, and the salvation he offers to mankind – formed the summation of Belloc's religious belief. He had little interest in the Old Testament: "an unedifying piece of tribal mythology."[18] Nor was he in any way interested in those who indulged in what he called 'Bibliolatry,' by which he meant "the literal interpretation of that book."[19] Again, words, even holy ones, are less powerful in the Bellocian mind than acts – central of all being Christ's sacrifice for the salvation of humanity.

Yet this response which we may consider emotional, Belloc found to be a wholly rational response to a real event – 'a thing.' He was not interested in charismatic outpourings of Christianity which he found 'repulsive' –

17 Wilson, A.N., Hilaire Belloc, Complete Verse (Pimlico 1991), p. 12
18 Speaight, *Life of Hilaire Belloc ibid*, p. 301
19 Belloc, Hilaire, *The Cruise of the Nona, ibid*, pp. 174 – 175

'good for others not for me.'[20] Sentimental religious poetry appalled him. A great amount of this type of verse appeared after the First World War and appealed to those who had lost loved ones in the conflict. Belloc had lost his own dear son and he was angered by attempts at emotional manipulation. Writing to Juliet Duff regarding a very popular poet of this genre, he declared that he "ought to be crushed to pulp in a mortar then drawn through a sieve."[21]

Another form of religious writing that became popular in the 1920s (and is surely even more popular today) was that which focused on the personal journey of the soul, tailor-made spiritual reflections and desires that put the individual at the centre of the cosmic tapestry. While crossing the Atlantic in 1923, Belloc met an "an elderly American woman" who was reading the works of the psychic and occultist Walter Winston Kenilworth, whose works, Belloc gathered, were becoming increasingly popular in the United States. Belloc asked if he could borrow the book. Having read it, he was eager to share its contents in one of his letters to his friend, Mrs Balfour:

> Here is one sentence, 'who has seen with the Mirror of the Enlightened Mind through which and in which the Self of the Soul is seen?' And here is another. 'Trust in the in-dwelling Self and have boundless faith in the Self-Soul and the Soul-Self.' There are 261 pages of it. He has written another book called *The Way to Power* – all Soul-stuff. It seems they [the Americans] wolf this sort of hay down like a herd of Donkeys ....[22]

Another very popular book at this time – on both sides of the Atlantic – was Sir James Frazer's *The Golden Bough* – that claimed to prove the existence of an enduring and very ancient religious system that had survived the imposition and repression of Christianity. Margaret Murray similarly sought to show the existence and endurance of a real witchcraft religion. Today, folklorists are highly sceptical of both writers and the numerous inconsistencies and exaggerations in their work have been

20 Speaight, *ibid*, p. 381
21 Speaight, Letters to Hilaire Belloc, *ibid*, letter to Juliet Duff, p. 144
22 Speaight, *ibid*, p. 131

discussed and amplified on many occasions. Belloc met Frazer once and recorded his impressions of the man he encountered:

> I have often noticed that people who write books which are interesting and yet show a lack of intellectual grip, turn out when one meets them in private life to be mad. It is perhaps their madness that starts them on their wild and interesting theories, and at the same time prevents them from exercising intellectual power, for a madman's writings never show intellectual grip and indeed a man of tenacious intellect is the opposite to a madman.

> This chap Frazer goes on precisely as I have seen lunatics go on in Asylums. He sits in a corner muttering and mumbling to himself with a terrified and surly look in his eye. His wife who leads him about is a sort of lion-tamer, and fears him no more than the hunter does the Denizen of the forest. But all others fear him and keep well out of reach of any sudden plunge with a cutting instrument. For my part the contrast between him and his book kept me in subdued laughter almost the whole time I was with him.[23]

There were those whose 'goodness' attracted Belloc, and in the presence of such people, he always showed the utmost respect and attention. Father Vincent McNabb was one such person. A man of both piety and learning, he helped Belloc through the most difficult periods of his life, including the death of his wife and his eldest son, when to carry on living seemed an impossible struggle. Belloc heaped praise on McNabb and all he represented, singling out his great virtues:

> The greatness of his character, of his learning, his experience, and, above all, his judgement, was altogether separate from the world about him … the most remarkable aspect of all was the character of holiness …. I can write here from intimate personal experience …. I have known, seen and felt holiness in [his] person … I have seen holiness at its full in the very domestic paths of my life, and the memory of that experience, which is also a vision, fills me as I write – so fills me that there is nothing now to say.[24]

23 Speaight, *Life of Hilaire Belloc, ibid,* pp. 431 – 432
24 Morton, *ibid.*

It would be wrong, however, to assume that deep love and respect for one priest was replicated into a general love for the Church and its members, as these two quotes should suffice to demonstrate:

> The Catholic Church is an institution I am bound to hold divine – but for unbelievers a proof of its divinity might be found in the fact that no merely human institution conducted with such knavish imbecility would have lasted a fortnight.[25]

Or this:

> I have been having my bellyful of clerics lately. I always like to associate with a lot of priests because it makes me understand anti-clerical things so well.[26]

The reader, at this point, might be wondering at the temerity and insolence of a man who called himself a Christian and claimed to believe in good things. There is a good deal of bluster and almost pantomime behaviour in some of Belloc's attitudes and observations. Much of his more outrageous comments were made in private letters to friends, rather than in published books and pamphlets. He exaggerated to prove a point and also to 'let off steam.' Those who knew him well understood this in him and accepted this hyperbole as what we might today call his 'coping mechanism.'

It could also be that this flippancy, this loud hectoring, disguised Belloc's own doubts? That his great solid foundation of faith had a crack in it and that crack was poised above a deep pit of despair? For this was a man who left us some short but bleak verses, suggesting little room for hope:

> In soft deluding lies let fools delight.
> A shadow marks our days; which end in Night.

25 Speaight, *ibid*, p. 383
26 *Ibid*

And:

> Loss and Possession, Death and Life are one.
> There falls no shadow where shines no sun.[27]

Once, when walking on the downs near Slindon, Belloc met a tramp. The two men talked and found that they had many things in common, especially in matters of spiritual understanding. The tramp shared with Belloc his lunch, which consisted of an onion, and Belloc, for his part, gave him all the change he could find in his pockets for a meal at The Cricketers Arms at Duncton, where the tramp was heading. As the man turned to leave, Belloc called him back:

> 'I wish,' I said with regret, 'we might meet and talk more often of many things. So much do we agree, and men like you and me are often lonely.' He shrugged his shoulders and put his head on one side, quizzing at me with his eyes. Then he shook his head decidedly, and said: 'No, no – it is certain that we shall never meet again,' And thanking me with great fervour, but briefly, he went largely and strongly down the escarpment of the Combe to Duncton and the weald; and I shall never see him again till the Great Day ....[28]

In this description, we see Belloc's willingness to talk with any man who would talk to him about the 'great things' and it was no concern to Belloc whether that person be of low or high birth. The encounter with the tramp reveals, once again, Belloc's spiritual naivety – his belief that all will ultimately be resolved on 'the Great Day,' when the redeemed will be reconciled with God. Belloc could talk of spiritual matters to a tramp or to one of his upper class friends, such as Katherine Asquith (with whom he probably discussed these matters more deeply than with anyone else), social status, here on earth, was of no consequence.

---

27 Wilson, *Collected Verse, ibid,* p. 119
28 Belloc, Hilaire, *The Hills and the Sea* (Methuen & Co, 1927, originally published, 1906) p. 224

The Supernatural

The existence of the supernatural world was not a contentious issue that vexed Belloc. He knew it existed, even if he couldn't explain it. There were things that could not be explained and for which no mortal person should seek explanation. As with the soul-searching of the American lady, he had no time or interest in examining the claims or counter claims of the unseen world or interrogating the truth or otherwise of paranormal events; he was content to believe that, through Christ, our journey from one life to the next will be completed without hazard or peril.

His ability to accept the occurrence of apparently inexplicable things, over which we have no control, led him to brush aside encounters with the supernatural much as he would a sudden rain shower or gust of wind. A striking example of this is related in A.N. Wilson's biography of Belloc. It was Belloc's practice to dictate his books rather than write them, and it was left to his poor secretaries, first Ruby Goldsmith, and later Bonnie Soames, to try and keep up with the rapid pace of his dictation. Wealthy friends would offer him rooms in their houses, so that he could work in peace and without distraction. During these sessions, Belloc focused his mind on the work in hand and nothing else. It is in this context that the incident related by Wilson took place:

> Bonnie Soames had the same experience, during work-hours, of this almost trance-like absorption. Once, when she had come over to Pixton [a country house owned by Belloc's friends, the Herberts] to help him finish a book, they sat alone together in the library. All the Herberts were out hunting, and there appeared to be no servants about either. Belloc began to dictate, as usual, firing words at her more rapidly than any pencil could scribble short-hand. After an hour or so of this, Miss Soames became aware of a hideous screaming noise from the next room, and she at length felt constrained to mention it.
>
> 'Mr Belloc, can you hear that noise?'
>
> 'Noise, my child?'
>
> 'It sounds like screaming.'

Pause, after which Belloc said, 'it is a boy screaming.'

'Well, Mr Belloc, don't you think we should investigate?'

They paced about the house, but the noise had died down. It was only when they returned to the library that the banshee-shriek once more assailed their ears. It began to dawn on Miss Soames that this was a case of the supernatural; they were not listening to a live gardener's boy being whipped; they were hearing something spectral. Once more they paced the house, and checked every room. It was only in the library that the screams could be heard, and yet no child was visible.

Miss Soames sat in her chair, shaken and alarmed.

'I don't think there is anything we can do about this,' said Belloc, who promptly went on with his dictation, his own voice drowning out that of the child's soul in torment. It provides a perfect example of his concentrated absorption in his work; and also, of how much for granted he took the absolute reality of the supernatural.[29]

In his book about Joan of Arc, Belloc totally accepts that her 'voices' were real and were transmitted from the spiritual realm. A modern historian or even a writer of fiction describing Joan would probably feel the need to suggest mental illness, or that the voices should be considered allegorical or were added by chroniclers at the time to discredit and demean her achievements. They would, very likely, be keen to reinvent her as a medieval feminist hero. Belloc had no such qualms and accepted her as one in communion with spirits, whose advice was far more credible than her mortal advisers, who begged her pause her relentless march against her enemies:

> But Joan was fevered at such lingering, knowing that she had but a year. Also her Voices bade her urgently to march; and the High Ones of Heaven are wiser than men.[30]

Belloc knew, or sensed, the power of an energetic world beyond that

---

29 Wilson, *Life of Hilaire Belloc, ibid*, p. 313
30 Belloc, Hilaire, *Joan of Arc* (Cassell & Company 1929), p. 96

perceived or understood by science. He was neither evangelical nor dogmatic in matters of religious belief, but he believed in the revelation of the risen Christ and he believed in the enduring quality of European civilisation. He also believed that the latter could not have been sustained without the existence of the Catholic Church.

The Spirit of the Sea

Belloc loved the sea as much as he loved the beauty of the land. For recreation, as we shall see later, he sailed, often alone, on a succession of old sailing boats ('yacht' would be far too grand a description). In *The Cruise of the Nona*, Belloc gives expression to his relationship to the sea and, once again, we see Belloc equate elemental forces with spiritual repose:

> There, on the sea, is a man nearest to his own making, and in communion with that from which he came and to which we shall return. For the wise men of very long ago have said, and it is true, that out of salt water all things came. The sea is the matrix of creation, and we have the memory of it in our blood.
>
> The sea has taken me to itself whenever I sought it and has given me relief from men. It has rendered remote the cares and wastes of the land; for of all the creatures that move and breathe upon earth, we of mankind are the fullest of sorrow. But the sea shall comfort us, and perpetually show us new things and assure us. It is the common sacrament of this world. May it be to others what it has been to me.

Belloc was capable of writing deep and complex poetry, but he could also write very simple verse; deceptively simple verse. One example is 'In a Boat,' which, I believe, he wrote after a close encounter with death in Bardsey Sound – a particularly treacherous piece of water that separates the Llyn Peninsula from Bardsey island (Ynys Enlli in Welsh). This part of Wales is deeply imbued with both Christian and pagan heritage. The peninsula has many ancient archaeological features, including standing

stones, megaliths, hill forts, and holy wells (springs); it also possesses two
ancient churches, both on the pilgrims' route to Bardsey – 'the island of
10,000 saints' in Christian mythology. Aberdaron is perched on the tip of
the peninsula; its old church clings to the hillside, perilously close to the
sea – it is a church that is seen by sailors successfully passing through
Bardsey Sound, heading for Abersoch or Pwilheli. In the mid-twentieth
century, the vicar here was R.S. Thomas, the celebrated Welsh poet, whose
verse echoed Belloc in many ways, although Thomas was more inclined to
doubt and despair in his poetry than Belloc.

'In a Boat' displays all the religious and spiritual facets of Belloc's
nature, as well as the huge importance he attached to the feminine in the
movement and life of the world, whether this be expressed in the person
of the Virgin Mary, or in his celestial queen, the moon.:

Lady! Lady!
Upon Heaven-height,
Above the harsh morning
In the mere light.

Above the spindrift
And above the snow,
Where no seas tumble,
And no winds blow.

The wind harries
And the cold kills;
But I see your chapel
Over far hills.

My body is frozen,
My soul is afraid:
Stretch out your hands to me,
Mother and maid.

Mother of Christ,
And Mother of me,
Save me alive
from the howl of the sea.

If you will Mother me
Till I grow old,
I will hang in your chapel
A ship of pure gold.[31]

In this poem, Belloc is more child than adult. Christ himself urged those who listened to him to 'be like little children' if they wished to pass into the heavenly realm. Belloc understood this implicitly. Perhaps we all become like little children when suddenly confronted with our mortality? There was much that was childlike and innocent in Belloc's faith or, as Wilson has suggested, like that of a simple peasant. Belloc knew that the pride of men, their wealth and their power, would be of no use to them when confronted with the reality of eternity, either with or without God: "Jesus Christ/ Thou child so wise/ Bless mine hands and fill my eyes/ And bring my soul to Paradise."[32]

A New Religion

In *The Cruise of the Nona*, Belloc contemplated the future and what future generations might expect to experience and he was not hopeful. He foresaw greed and obsessive individualism becoming rampant. He thought Darwinian ideas of Natural Selection and 'survival of the fittest' were creating a dangerous delusion that some races and some people were innately superior to others:

> He begins to make a new religion and a new mythology for himself to talk of an 'Ascent of Man,' he thinks himself a summit and a glory – and at the same time rids himself of morals.[33]

The first chapter of this book opened with Ernest Hemingway and his friends confusing Belloc with Aleister Crowley, the occultist and self-

31 Wilson, *Collected Verse, ibid*, p. 39 – 40
32 *Ibid*, p. 38
33 Belloc, Hilaire, *The Cruise of the Nona, ibid*, p. 125

styled promoter of 'magick.' It is very interesting to read what Crowley was writing around the time that Belloc was issuing his warnings:

> On the Christian hypothesis the reality of evil makes the devil equal to God [and if I had to take sides, then] it was not difficult to make up my mind. The forces of good were those which had constantly oppressed me. I saw them daily destroying the happiness of my fellow men. Since, therefore it was my business to experience the spiritual world, my first step must be to get into personal communion with the devil.[34]

Like Belloc, Crowley had a tendency to shock, so not all his statements should be taken at face value, however there was no doubting his core beliefs. He is best remembered for his dictums, "do what thou wilt shall be the whole of the law," and "every man and woman is a star." In other words, do not be held back by moral constraints, but do what your will desires, or as Hollywood westerns had it, "a man's gotta do what a man's gotta do." The second dictum seems harmless enough – but is it? If every man and every woman really believes they are a star shining in the universe, what are the consequences of such thinking? In the 1960s, Andy Warhol said "everyone will be famous for fifteen minutes," and with the popularity of 'Reality TV', this prediction seems to have become true. More than that we see people preoccupied with issues of identity and self-image as never before.

Crowley believed that Christianity was finished and would be replaced by what he very humbly called 'Crowleyanity,' a world where all intentions and desires would be pursued unhindered by nasty, clinging, debilitating morality: "My own attitude was unhampered by any ethical considerations," he declared, "ordinary morality is for ordinary people."[35] It could be argued we live far more in the world of Aleister Crowley than we do in the world of Hilaire Belloc, something that Belloc himself foresaw:

---

34 Wilson, Colin, *Aleister Crowley, The Nature of the Beast* (The Aquarian Press 1987), p. 40
35 Wilson, Colin *ibid*, p. 54

What I think will spring out of the filth is a new religion .... This conception of a new religion (and therefore an evil one) arising out of the grave of truth, seems today [1925] at once fantastic and unpleasant. Unpleasant I admit it is; fantastic I do not believe it to be.[36]

Belloc and Crowley were very similar men: forceful, powerful, and unafraid of public ridicule or censure. The difference was that Crowley sought spiritual ecstasy in the expansion and glory of the self, while Belloc understood the spiritual benefits of humility, which is why he revered 'simple men' like Tommy Pope, Stephen Reynolds and Father Vincent McNabb: "Blessed is he that has come to the heart of the world and is humble."[37]

Despite his Catholicism, Belloc was not blind to the literary merits of those with whom he differed theologically or ideologically. John Milton, for example, may have "died disbelieving the omnipotence of his creator, the divinity of his Saviour and the native immortality of mankind,"[38] but Belloc regarded *Paradise Lost* as one of the greatest examples of spiritual verse ever written:

For indeed Milton's effect is the effect of a voice once somewhere passionately loved, now heard again, and recalling beatitude. He that has ears for the poetic revelation knows how truly it proclaims itself over and over again in the luxuriant forest of 'Paradise Lost.' He that has appreciation for form feels the strength of form perpetually as he reads; he that knows what landscape can do for the mind is granted in 'Paradise Lost,' vision of such landscape as we hardly find in the real world.[39]

Spiritual energy is, for some, no more than a superstitious fantasy, for which no scientific evidence exists. For men like Crowley and Belloc its existence was beyond doubt. Mary Shelley forever remembered today as

---

36 Belloc, *The Cruise of the Nona, ibid*, p. 129
37 Wilson, A.N., *Complete Verse*, p. 38
38 Belloc, Hilaire, *Milton* (Cassell & Company, 1935), p. 309
39 *Ibid*, p. 261

the author of 'Frankenstein,' lived an early life bedevilled by tragedy. That life was shaped and directed by her husband, Percy Bysshe Shelley, a man who believed very much as Crowley believed, and lived very much as Crowley lived. Looking back on those days in middle age, Mary Shelley rejected the sensuality and individualism she had embraced as a young woman:

> I believe we are sent here to educate ourselves, and that self-denial, and disappointment, and self-control, are part of our education, that it is not by taking away all restraining law that our improvement is to be achieved.[40]

Belloc would have heartily agreed with those sentiments.

---

40 Sampson, Fiona, *In Search of Mary Shelley, The Girl Who Wrote Frankestain* (Profile Books 2018), p. 235

'The Four Men'

MYSTERIOUS LANDSCAPES AND THE SEARCH FOR HOME

An unconscious or fated combination: the archetype of the triad, which
calls for the fourth to complete it ….

CARL JUNG

A Place in which to Belong

This chapter is given over to just one of Belloc's books, *The Four Men*. In
old age, Belloc lamented that "I put my whole soul into that book, but no
one reads it now."[1] Belloc scholars have long agreed that this was one of his
seminal works. The *Path to Rome* fizzes with youthful exuberance, just as
The Cruise of the Nona, written 23 years later, is full of rueful reflection
and the 'gathering up' of later life. *The Four Men*, written in 1912, sits
between these two contrasting periods, and, it could be argued, is Belloc at
his best, before bereavement and age began to sap his vitality.

It is a book dedicated to the county of Sussex, in the preface, Belloc
addresses the county as if it possessed personality and were a living thing.
Here, he explains, he finds "the character of enduring things," yet he senses
time and modernity acting to erode all that he treasures and loves about
the county:

> In this love he [Belloc] remains content until, perhaps, some sort of warning
> reaches him, that even his own County is approaching its doom. Then,
> believe me, Sussex, he is anxious in a very different way; he would, if he
> could, preserve his land in the flesh, and keep it there as it is, forever. But

---

1   Belloc, Elizabeth, quoted by Robert Speaight, The *Life of Hilaire Belloc* (Hollis &
    Carter 1957), p. 328

since he knows he cannot do that, 'at least,' he says, 'I will keep her image, and that shall remain.' And as a man will paint with peculiar passion a face which he is only permitted to see for a little time, so will one passionately set down one's own horizon and one's fields before they are forgotten and have become a different thing. Therefore it is that I have put down in writing what happened to me now so many years ago, when I first met one man and then another, and we four bound ourselves and walked through all your land, Sussex, from end to end.[2]

We will consider later whether this was indeed a walk that Belloc actually undertook and whether he actually met and walked with the companions he describes. All is not what it seems in *The Four Men*. What is clear is that the book is an elegy, and that, to some extent, Sussex is a metaphor for home, exile, and the hope of a better life to come. These three themes occur constantly in Belloc's writings, but in none of his other writings are they so fulsomely explored nor so vividly portrayed. The device of four companions, all of different ages and personality, allows Belloc to slip effortlessly from reality to fantasy, from profundity to humour, and all set out against the background of the Sussex landscape in late autumn.

Exile is for Belloc a real thing, something he knew and experienced, probably every day of his life. In part this was born from his alienation from the religious and political life of the country he was living in, and that itself emanated from the mixed loyalty of his Anglo-French upbringing. J.B. Morton understood these constantly shifting sands of Belloc's personality more than most:

His wit was French, but his humour English. He was profoundly moved by the beauty of English landscape, but preferred the French way of living. His military temper, his love of justice rather than order, the logical process of his thought were French. At sea he was English, but Irish in that recurring dream of a landfall which is not of this world.[3]

---

2   Belloc, Hilaire, *The Four Men*, A Farrago (Thomas Nelson and Sons, 1911), preface.
3   Morton, J.B., *Hilaire Belloc, A Memoir* (Hollis & Carter 1955), pp. 3–4

His sense of being a Frenchman compelled him to undertake his year of national service in the French Army as a young man, not something he had to do, as he was living in England. In future years, Belloc made much of the camaraderie and sense of belonging that he experienced in those days, but we may wonder how accepted this Englishman was among his fellows, and the degree to which he could fully engage in their conversations and repartee. Especially in provincial France, where the language and accent was very different from the French he knew, he could feel very alone, as he recalled:

> That night I sat at a peasant's table and heard my four stable-companions understanding everything, and evidently in their world and at home, although they were conscripts. This turned me silent, and I sat away from the light, looking at the fire, and drying myself by its logs. As I heard their laughter I remembered Sussex and the woods above Arun, and I felt myself to be in exile.[4]

In *The Hills and The Sea*, published two years before *The Four Men*, Belloc returns continuously to the Sussex countryside and the Sussex people in his writing. He describes an inn, remote from the main roads and the general traffic of men, and the old Sussex couple who have run it for many years. All is good with the inn and with its hosts. Here is indeed a place where Belloc could feel at home:

> … it was quite dark, and the windows, with their square, large panes and true proportions, shone out and made it home. The room within received me like a friend. The open chimney at its end, round which the house was built was filled with beech logs burning; and the candles, which were set in brass, mixed their yellow light with that of the fire. The long ceiling was low, as are the ceilings of Heaven. And oak was everywhere also: in the beams and the shelves and the mighty table.[5]

Beech is the wood of the Sussex downs and oak the timber of the Sussex

4   Speaight, Robert, The *Life of Hilaire Belloc* (Hollis & Carter 1957), p. 73
5   Belloc, Hilaire, *The Hills and the Sea* (Thomas Nelson 1910), pp. 277 – 278

weald – here they combine in Belloc's 'heaven.' For such a holy setting, it was necessary that a sort of communion feast should be brought to him:

> When they put food and ale before me, it was of the kind which has been English ever since England began, and which perhaps good fortune will preserve over the breakdown of our generation, until we have England back again. One could see the hops in the tankard, and one could taste the barley, until, more and more sunk into the plenitude of the good house, one could dare to contemplate, as though from a distant standpoint, the corruption and the imminent danger of the time through which we must lead our lives. And, as I so considered the ruin of the great cities and their slime, I felt as though I were in a sort of fortress of virtue and of health ….[6]

Even here, Belloc is not really at home. He is hiding from the real England of cities and capitalism, of motor cars and advertising hoardings. What is more, these old Sussex country people were not his people – much as he wished they could be – they were, simply beyond his cultural reach. Writing fifteen years later, Belloc admitted as much, and that both he and his near neighbour at Shipley, Wilfrid Scawen Blunt, could never be 'of Sussex,' however much they wished they could:

> I had lived among them on and off all my life, and so had he; and I certainly love them with all my heart and so did he; but as for knowing how they live or what they really think, there is a gulf between us.[7]

The Four Men is set on very specific dates. It begins on 29th October 1902 and ends on 2nd November 1902. Yet there is no evidence that Belloc was out walking on those days, nor that he met the companions he describes sharing the journey with. We must conclude that the idea of the walk first entered his imagination on those days and remained, constant in his imagination, until he had space and time to compose and write all he had imagined. There is a hint of the book to come in one of his essays in *The Hills and The Sea*:

6 *Ibid*, p. 278
7 Belloc, Hilaire, *The Cruise of the Nona* (Constable & Co 1955, originally published, 1925), p. 119

It is no wonder, then, that at this peculiar time, this week (or moment of the year), the desires which if they do not prove at least demand – perhaps remember – our destiny, come strongest. They are proper to the time of autumn, and all men feel them. The air is at once new and old; the morning (if one rises early enough to welcome its leisurely advance) contains something in it of profound reminiscence. The evenings hardly yet suggest (as they soon will) friends and security, and the fires of home. The thoughts awakened in us by their bands of light fading along the downs are thoughts which go with loneliness and prepare me for the isolation of the soul. It is on this account that tradition has set, at the entering of autumn, for a watch at the gate of the season, the Archangel; and at its close the day and the night of All-Hallows on which the dead return.[8]

The Four Men is a very different book to *The Path to Rome*, with which it is often compared. It is confined to a much smaller geographical area than *The Path to Rome* – the county of Sussex. Yet, at the same time it jour-neys much further than *The Path to Rome* – exploring the mystical and unseen world and the destiny of man. Belloc's chosen vehicle for this odys-sey is the chance meeting of four men. These travelling companions never reveal their real names but confer on each other descriptive epithets that most clearly describe their personalities. There is Grizzlebeard, The Sailor, and The Poet. The narrator – Belloc – is simply called 'Myself' – "for that is the name I shall give to my own person and my own soul". From the first pages, the reader is made aware that this is no ordinary travel book or nov-el and these are no ordinary men. Belloc subtitled his book 'a farrago', which the dictionary tells us means a 'confused mixture'. Although the reader may indeed at times be confused, Belloc was very clear in his inten-tion of exploring all those things in life that to him seemed important and necessary.

It is helpful to see what Belloc's biographers thought of *The Four Men*. All three make the link between *The Four Men*, published in 1912, and *The Path to Rome*, published ten years earlier. Writing in 1957 – only four years after Belloc's death – Robert Speaight observes that whereas "*The Path to*

8   Belloc, *Hills and the Sea*, ibid, p. 289

Rome was a pilgrimage, *The Four Men* is an exploration". It is "the mixture of the real with the imaginary that gives the book its unique flavour".[9]

A.N. Wilson agrees, commenting that *The Four Men* is different, "more poignantly elegiac, more hauntingly religious".[10] Joseph Pearce, Belloc's most recent biographer, believes that in writing *The Four Men*, Belloc "provided a metaphysical path through Sussex to accompany his path to Rome, a secular pilgrimage conveying a soul's love for the soil of his native home". Both Rome and Sussex are holy places and, as a result "*The Four Men* is full of spiritual premonitions of 'the character of enduring things' amid the decay of time".[11]

Enlightening as these observations are, they obscure the humour that is central to the book. Belloc may have thought deeply about matters both material and divine, but he also drank deeply as well, and when drinking he liked to sing songs, which he admitted could be lewd, loud and blasphemous. Just as there was day and night – life and death – so, for Belloc, profundity had to be balanced by levity. This coming at life from two directions simultaneously was the Bellocian way. He found "the goodness of God in the drinking of ale, which is a kind of prayer," and added, "drinking good ale is a more renowned and glorious act than any other to which a man can lend himself".[12]

Belloc wrote many songs in the folk song idiom. As a young man, living in Sussex, he would have heard songs being sung by men working in the fields or groups of men singing in inns or at country fairs. *The Four Men* is peppered with these songs, ranging from The Sailor's Carol ("rank blasphemy", as Grizzlebeard calls it), to a song about Duke William of Normandy, to the very surreal 'His Hide is Covered in Hair'. Belloc delighted friends and family with his impromptu rendition of these songs, which, more often than not, were sustained by a tankard or two of good ale!

---

9   Speaight, *ibid*, p. 326
10 Wilson, A.N., *Hilaire Belloc* (Hamish Hamilton 1984), p. 111
11 Pearce, Joseph, *Old Thunder, A Life of Hilaire Belloc* (Harper Collins, 2002), p. 87
12 Belloc, Hilaire, *The Four Men, ibid*, p. 256

Meeting the Four Men

We are introduced to each of the four characters in turn. The book opens with Myself, sitting in the George pub at Robertsbridge, "drinking that port of theirs," as he waits, possibly for a train, to take him on "some business", "not even for ambition or for adventure, but only to earn". It is then he decides that as he is on the soil of his native Sussex and with "Kent a mile or two behind," he will walk towards the west and his home by way of the Arun valley. In his mind he resolves to get up and go back to his home, if only for one day. He slams his hand on the table, exclaiming, "I will go from this place to my home." He is then surprised to hear the deeper voice of an older man replying: "And since I am going to that same place, let us journey there together." Thinking himself to be alone, Myself is surprised and angry at the interruption, but the old man explains that he too wishes to travel to that part of Sussex. "A man is more himself if he is one of a number; so let us take the road together, and, as we go, gather what company we can find." This is Grizzlebeard, who we learn is a tall, vigorous man, though "well on in years." His eyes are deep set and "full of travel and of sadness." His hair is curled and plentiful and "the colour of steel," as is his beard.[13]

Grizzlebeard and Myself meet their next companion at the inn at Brightling:

> We found there a very jovial fellow with a sort of ready smile behind his face, and eyes that were direct and keen. But these eyes were veiled with the salt of the sea, and paler than the eyes of a landsman would have been; for by the swing of his body as he sat there, and the ease of his limbs, he was a sailor.[14]

With the Sailor as the third companion, they meet the fourth on the road and quickly ascertain who this man may be:

> We watched the man before us more closely, and we saw that as he walked his long limbs seemed to have loose joints, his arms dangled rather than

13 *ibid*, pp. 4–5
14 *ibid*, p. 15

swang, he steered no very straight course along the road, and under his felt hat with its narrow brim there hung tawny hair much too long, and in no way vigorous. His shirt was soft, grey and dirty, and of wool, and his collar made one with it, the roll of which peeped above his throat, and his coat was velveteen, like a [game] keeper's, but he was not like a keeper in any other way, and no one would have trusted him with a gun .… Then we saw him stop suddenly, pull a pencil out of some pocket or other, and feel about in several more for some paper as we supposed. 'I am right,' said Grizzlebeard in triumph. 'He is a Poet!'[15]

The Poet, Sailor and Grizzlebeard are already on their journey. It is Myself who changes his plans. Even though it would seem that the other three join him, it is he who joins them. Renowned psychoanalyst Carl Jung has written of "the archetype of the triad, which calls for the fourth to complete it,"[16] suggesting that Belloc, however unconsciously, was tapping into a profound symbolism.

Myself comes from the world of work and conformity, Grizzlebeard represents the wisdom of years, while the Poet represents the naivety of youth. The Sailor stands for freedom: "You must not be surprised if I go off by this road or by that at any hour, without your leave or any other man's; for so long as I have money in my pocket I am determined to see the world."[17]

It has been suggested that the four men are all aspects of Belloc's own personality. He is journeying alone but the different aspects of his personality are alive within him. When Belloc was a young man he wished to be a poet. Indeed he wrote much verse throughout his life but he never really believed he wrote as good a verse as he would have wished. For relaxation, Belloc sailed the coast of England in his yacht, the *Nona*. As an old man he sported a great beard, and although wearied by personal loss (his wife and both his sons died when still young) and increasing poor health, he never lost his courteous manner or sense of fun.

---

15 *Ibid*, p. 25
16 Jung, C.G., *Memories, Dreams, Reflection* (Pantheon Books, 1963), p. 289
17 Belloc, *ibid*, p. 16

Jung might almost have been writing of Belloc when he described the personality type that takes "further steps along the road" than other men. "He will go alone," wrote Jung, "and be his own company. He will serve as his own group, consisting of a variety of opinions and tendencies – which need not necessarily be marching in the same direction. In fact he will be at odds with himself." Such a man, Jung concluded, will seek solace in his surroundings as a defence against "his inner multiplicity."[18] The landscape of Sussex – its hills and rivers, its market towns and villages were, for Belloc, the port in the storm of life. As he travelled around the world for work, sometimes being absent for more months of the year than he was at home, that very home became his anchor amidst the "ever changeful sea" of life.

The Landscape of *The Four Men*

As the four men talk and walk, they pass through the High Weald of eastern Sussex with "its little pointed hills", and into the South Downs that dominate the western part of the county. We are always reminded that the landscape is ancient and rooted in the history of past generations:-

> So all along the road we went under Chanctonbury, that high hill, we went as the morning broadened: along a way that is much older than anything in the world …. By that way we went, by walls and trees that seemed as old as the old road itself, talking of all those things men talk of, because men were made for speech and for companionship ….[19]

The landscape is almost a fifth companion and the cause of much discussion and reflection among the four travellers. There is one memorable moment in the book, when Myself beholds the full moon rising over Chanctonbury on Hallowe'en. We are invited to see a mystical interaction taking place between the ancient hilltop and the 'holy moon' shining down on its prehistoric features. Belloc, the Catholic, often seems more like Belloc, the pagan.

18 Jung, *ibid*, p. 376
19 Belloc, *ibid*, pp. 160 – 161

This beloved landscape was indeed a home to Belloc – a spiritual as well as a physical home. As they approach the end of their journey, they stop one last time to drink and sing in a country inn. "I knew myself indeed to be still in my own county", says Myself, "and I was glad inside my heart, like a man who hears the storm upon the window, but is himself housed by the fire..."[20]

There were some parts of Sussex that Belloc thought were best avoided. These were towns of "the London sort", by which he meant Burgess Hill and Haywards Heath, and would certainly have included Brighton too, had that town been on their route. These towns had grown up with the railway and represented a dramatic interruption in the slow pace of rural life. This was the "detestable part of the county, which was not made for men, but rather for tourists or foreigners, or London people that had lost their way".[21]

The sky above the landscape is a recurring theme in *The Four Men*, particularly the sky at dusk, a vivid sight "full of departure and of rest". On approaching Henfield one evening, the four men are deep in conversation and then they see that the day is passing as they walk towards the setting sun:

> The sky was already of an apple green to the westward, and in the eastern blue there were stars. There also shone what had not yet appeared on that windless day, a few small wintry clouds, neat and defined in heaven. Above them, the moon, past her first quarter but not yet full, was no longer pale, but began to make a cold glory; and all that valley of Adur was a great solemn sight to see as we went forward upon our adventure that led nowhere and away. To us four men, no one of whom could know the other, and who had met by I could not tell what chance, and would part very soon for ever, these things were given. All four of us together received the sacrament of that wide and silent beauty, and we ourselves went in silence to receive it.

---

20 Belloc *ibid*, p. 286
21 Belloc, *ibid*, p. 46

The Philosophy of *The Four Men*

The philosophy of *The Four Men* finds its expression in the landscape, where the spiritual and the everyday come together as one: "… if a man is part of and is rooted in one steadfast piece of earth , which has nourished him and given him his being, and if he can on his side lend it glory and do it service, it will be a friend to him for ever, and he has outflanked Death in a way."[22]

The elemental forces of life that caused philosophers to pause and consider at length could, for Belloc, be exemplified in a simple domestic chore, such as the boiling of a kettle:

> I woke next morning to the noise, the pleasant noise, of water boiling in a kettle. May God bless that noise and grant it to be the most sacred noise in the world. For it is the noise that babes hear at birth and that old men hear as they die in their beds, and it is the noise of our households all our long lives long; and throughout the world, wherever men have hearths, that purring and that singing, and that humming and that talking to itself of warm companionable water to our great ally, the fire, is home.[23]

Everything comes in its season and none can escape the turning of the year and the passing of time. All Hallows falls on November 1st, which, Belloc notes, nicely balances out "All Fools", seven months earlier, on April 1st, when the year "is light and young, and when she has forgotten winter and is glad that summer is near, and has never heard the name of autumn at all, or of the fall of the leaves". Belloc would have been familiar with the folk song "The Life of a Man", that speaks of man's life being no more than the leaves on the tree, that will be "beautiful and bright" one day and then be withered by the frost and blown away by the storm.

The Bellocian philosophy, although profound, was not inclined to self-indulgence. At one point in the book, Grizzlebeard gets into a long and heated argument with a philosopher whom he meets in a pub. The 'balderdash' conversation is brought to a sudden conclusion when the

---

22 Belloc, *ibid*, p. 309
23 Belloc, *ibid*, pp. 71 – 72

Sailor 'baptises' the philosopher by pouring a tankard of ale over his head. Think, by all means, says Belloc, but not for too long. Comradeship is gained by doing rather than thinking: "men become companionable by working with their bodies and not with their weary noodles, and the spinning out of stuff from oneself is an inhuman thing".[24]

Humour of *The Four Men*

Eighteen pages of *The Four Men* are given over to a long description of "the Great War between Sussex and Kent." At first the reader imagines that he is learning of an epic conflict from medieval times, although he is not left in any doubt that the tale is very tongue-in-cheek and very much told at the expense of Kent, whose king is described as an irascible illiterate! However the age of knights in armour is soon dispelled, as Myself describes how the men of Sussex belaboured the men of Kent with ash sticks and herded them down to the level crossing over the railway at Brede, where "the little man in green corduroy who kept the level crossing" allowed them to cross – the Sussex men sending the men of Kent scattering in all directions. The war, we are told, all came about because the Kentish folk had purloined a Sussex song and called it their own – a grave offence!

The story is great fun and very amusing, but in case it all seems like a figment of Belloc's imagination, a letter published in the *West Sussex Gazette* in 1957 suggested that battles on the Sussex/ Kent border were very real at the time *The Four Men* was set in 1902. The letter also highlights the reality of Sussex particularism, and its determination to keep up local traditions:

> … until this century the county was always markedly different in almost every aspect from the rest of England, and its exclusiveness produced a particularly strong local patriotism that evidenced itself in frequent week-end battles with 'foreigners' on its frontiers, particularly with the men of Kent, who, even when I was a boy, were still regarded much as Frenchmen and Germans were.[25]

24 Belloc, *ibid*, p. 238
25 *West Sussex Gazette*, 30th May 1957

The main humour in the book is found in the dialogues between the Sailor and the Poet. With the former forever deprecating the Poet's verse, while praising his own efforts in this regard. The Sailor is forever playfully boastful, declaring on one occasion that the song he is about to sing "is of a good loud roaring sort .... and you must know that it is more than one thousand years old". It had in all probability been composed that very day!

After lamenting one of the Poet's lyrical efforts, the Sailor declares that he must be a vegetarian and that like most "men of your luxury" he was probably afraid of his body, which was, the Sailor noted, "a lanky thing". To which Myself added a denunciation of all "water-drinkers also, and caterwauling outers, and turnip mumblers, enemies of beef, treasonable the immemorial ox and the traditions of our human kind!"

Another exchange sees the penniless Poet mocked for his penury as the four men sit down to eat and drink in another Sussex inn:-

The Poet: In the matter of eating and drinking I am with you all, but in the matter of paying I differ from you altogether, for I have nothing.

Myself: How is this, Poet? It was only today that I saw you with my own eyes at the Bluebell paying for a mug of beer with a labouring man.

The Poet: It was my last money, and I did it for charity.

The Sailor: Then you must have the reward of charity and starve.[26]

The Poet is again the butt of the joke when he suggests they could eat "some kind of cheese", to which Myself in mock horror tells him that in Sussex there is only one kind of cheese:

In Sussex, let me tell you, we have but one cheese, the name of which is CHEESE. It is One; and undivided, though divided into a thousand fragments, and unchanging, though changing in place and consumption. There is in Sussex no Cheese but Cheese, and it is the same true Cheese from the head of the Eastern Rother to Harting Hill, and from the sea-beach

26 Belloc, *ibid*, pp. 279 – 280

to that part of Surrey which we gat from the Marches with sword and bow. In colour it is yellow, which is the right colour of Cheese. It is neither young nor old. Its taste is that of cheese, and nothing more. A man may live upon it all the days of his life.[27]

Here is the devout Catholic, Belloc, parodying the Holy Sacrament. But then this was the same Belloc who, on being challenged by a group of rationalists as to how he could possibly believe the Jesuits when they told him that the Holy Communion bread turned into the flesh of Christ and the wine into his blood, responded by saying, "If they told me it turned into elephant's droppings, I would believe them!"[28] Belloc often shocked his co-religionists as much as he did the sceptics.

Heroes and Villains

Reading *The Four Men*, Belloc's dislike of other people becomes apparent. He disliked lawyers and politicians and especially the new rich whom he saw encroaching in every direction. He also had little time for the police, whom he saw as the servants of the rich. Several times, the four men pass through woods that were private property but through which the Sailor knew little-known paths they could take "so the servants of the rich could do us no hurt".[29] It is also stated that a man must be careful if he sings as he walks in the open countryside, as the police will arrest him as a vagabond. The poor say that the rich are wicked and since they are the great majority of men they are "likely to be right".[30]

Myself recounts the story of 'Peter the Politician', who tries to sell his soul, but is forever being frustrated in his attempt by a series of ever inferior Devils. Eventually, Peter the Politician, in anger and frustration, storms out of hell, leaving his soul behind, thus, he loses rather than sells his soul.[31]

27 Belloc, *ibid*, pp. 281 – 283
28 Wilson, *ibid*,
29 Belloc, *ibid*, p. 76
30 *Ibid*, p. 268
31 *Ibid*, pp. 268 – 275

We are introduced to the incredibly pompous Lord Justice Honybubble: "the constant exercise of bullying men who could not reply had given him a commanding manner".[32]

But the real villain of *The Four Men* is the 'Hideous Being', who turns out to be very rich indeed and by far the most odious person they meet on their journey:-

> He had a lump which was not his fault, and a sour look that was. He was smoking a long churchwarden pipe through his sneering lips. There was very little hair on his face, though he did not shave, and the ear turned towards us, the left ear, had been so broken that it looked pointed, and made one shudder. The sneer on his lips was completed by the long slyness of his eye. His legs were as thin as sticks, and he had one crossed over the other; his boots had elastic sides to them, and horrible tags fore and aft, and above them were measly grey socks thin and wrinkled. He did not turn or greet us as we appeared.[33]

It is the appearance of these wonderfully distorted, even monstrous characters, that so grabs the imagination of the reader and why the book lends itself so well to dramatic representation. Ann Feloy has adapted *The Four Men* for theatre, with variants of the original production being staged over the years, most recently in 2017, when it played to packed houses in venues across southern England.

Belloc was a great believer in courtesy and in treating people with good manners. During their journey, the four men entertained the labouring men they met in the pubs that they visited and paid for their beer "because we were better off than they".[34]

The poor are, in a sense, the heroes of *The Four Men* – it is their songs that cheer, their beer that quenches the thirst, and their eggs, bacon and cheese that sustain the four companions. But the one man who stands out for praise is John 'Mad Jack' Fuller, Squire of Brightling in the early nineteenth century. Fuller was a maverick Tory MP, who spent much of his

32 *Ibid*, p. 247
33 *Ibid*, pp. 145 – 152
34 *Ibid*, pp. 17 – 18

personal wealth on putting the local unemployed to work. He loved to eat and he loved to drink. He was suspended from the House of Commons for insulting the Speaker and after he died he was buried in a pyramid in Brightling churchyard. Myself tells us that Fuller lived in a "roaring way":

> He spent all his great fortune upon the poor of Sussex and of his own parish, bidding them drink deep and eat hearty as being the best preservative of life, until at last he died. There is the story of Fuller of Brightling, and may we all deserve as well as he.[35]

An End

At the end of *The Four Men*, it seems as if Myself's travelling companions may not have been ordinary men at all, but spirits, or conjured-up aspects of Belloc's own personality: "But as I walked along I looked furtively first to one side and then to the other … and it seemed to me (whether from the mist or what not) that they were taller than men; and their eyes avoided my eyes". Grizzlebeard declares that he and his two companions must now leave Myself this side of the border with Hampshire: "when he had said this, I was confused to wonder from his voice and from the larger aspect of himself and his companions, whether indeed they were men".[36]

Myself strains his eyes in the mist as he watches them disappear into the enveloping mist. He walks, bereft, high up onto the Downs and writes poetry to ease his mind, concluding:

> So, therefore, though myself be crosst
> The shuddering of that dreadful day
> When friend and fire and home are lost
> And even children drawn away –
> The passer-by shall hear me still,
> A boy that sings on Duncton Hill.[37]

---

35 *Ibid*, pp. 17 – 18
36 *Ibid*, p. 301
37 *Ibid* p. 309

Relieved by this poetical release, Myself heads southward "through the gathering darkness" to his home. It is clear that this home is the home to be found after Death as well as a physical home, and as such is a comfort to both the writer and his readers too.

In 1911, Belloc knew very well that the day might come "when the holy place shall perish and all the people of it,"[38] yet he still hoped that the Sussex he knew as a child might still endure: its clear, peaceful, open downland, its indomitable people, and its continuity with ages past. By 1936, he had abandoned all hope. Belloc was getting old by this time and although still vigorously fighting for the causes he believed in, he retained little expectation of success. It is in this context that we should read his gloomy assessment:

> Which of us could have thought, when we wandered, years ago, in the full peace of the summer weald, or through the sublime void of the high Downs, that the things upon which we had been nourished since first we could take joy in the world would be thus rapidly destroyed in our own time, dying even before we ourselves should die? Yet apparently it has come. In the old days when the huge amorphous mass of London, more numerous than many a state, was only linked with the sea-coast by the railway, we feared for the future, but did not despair of it. The coast might become a line of alien buildings, and here and there upon the main arteries across the weald some suburban thing having no fellowship with the county at all would grow up round a station; but Sussex as a whole remained untainted by the intrusion. The contrast between the meaningless new watering places, the suburban blotches and the ancient plough land, woodland, downland, was only the stronger.

> Then came the change: London broke out like a bursting reservoir, flooding all the ways to the sea, swamping our history and our past, so that already we are hardly ourselves. Of a week-end the roads from north to south are like a city street. The new engines climb the Downs; they invade every corner. You may hear the machine-gun fire of a motor bicycle on the greensward of Chanctonbury Ring. There is no retreat wherein you can

38 *Ibid*, preface, p. xix

escape the blind inhuman mechanic clatter. How could any organism survive this ubiquitous thrusting into its substance of alien things?[39]

In his poem, 'Ha'nacker Mill', written on the eve of the First World War, Belloc had seen, almost as a premonition, the calamities that would befall both him personally and the country as a whole. He was visiting his mother in Slindon, and was appalled and shocked to see that Halnacker Windmill – a place he loved to walk to and sit by when a boy, had been blown down in a storm. It brought tears to his eyes and soon these verses came to his mind, which seem, with hindsight, to be an elegy for an England that was on the threshold of oblivion:

Sally is gone that was so kindly
Sally is gone from Ha'nacker Hill.
And the Briar grows ever since then so blindly
And ever since then the clapper is still,
And the sweeps have fallen from Ha'nacker Mill.

Ha'nacker Hill is in Desolation:
Ruin a-top and a field unploughed.
And Spirits that call on a fallen nation
Spirits that loved her calling aloud:
Spirits abroad in a windy cloud.

Spirits that call and no one answers;
Ha'nacker's down and England's done.
Wind and Thistle for pipe and dancers
And never a ploughman under the Sun.
Never a ploughman. Never a one.[40]

---

39   Belloc, Hilaire, *The County of Sussex* (Cassell, 1936), pp. 202 – 203
40   Wilson, A.N. (Ed), *Hilaire Belloc, Complete Verse* (Pimlico 1991), p. 64

Belloc as a young child.

Belloc's mother Elizabeth, often known as Bessie.

Belloc on his arrival in Rome, 1901.

Belloc's wife Elodie in 1896.

The Alps, where Belloc saw his 'religion' [photo courtesy Paul Deacon].

Devil's Dyke, on Belloc's beloved South Downs, in 1885 [Sussex Archaeolgical Society].

Belloc's children, photographed at Kinsland (Two of his sons would die fighting for their country [West Sussex Record Office].

'Never a ploughman under the sun, never a ploughman, never a one' [Sussex Archaeolgical Society].

Belloc during his time at Oxford.

The Member of Parliament for Salford South (1905–10) [West Sussex Record Office].

Stolid Belloc: ready for the fight!

Belloc in his sixties, still working as hard as ever [West Sussex Record Office].

Cider makers at Lodsworth, Belloc loved singing the drinking songs he learned from the Sussex country people [Garland Collection, West Sussex Record Office].

Two old Sussex rustics, Upperton near Petworth, *c.*1930. Belloc loved the country people, though he could 'never know them' [Garland Collection, West Sussex Record Office].

Belloc on the 'Nona', c.1914.

Belloc still sailing in his sixties.

'The Beast', Aleister Crowley once mistaken for Belloc. The two men had personality traits in common, but very differtent spiritual convictions.

Lady Juliet Duff, the subject of Belloc's platonic infatuation in later life.

Katherine Asquith, Belloc corresponded at length with her on matters of theology and belief.

Belloc in his dotage.

George Bernard Shaw, Belloc and G. K. Chesterton.

75

Ross Muir and Emily Longhurst bringing alive the stroy of Hilaire Belloc to the children of Rusper School, 2019, as part of the Belloc, Broadwood and Beyond project. Writer and Belloc enthusiast, Rev Nick Flint vicar of Rusper, can be seen on the right.

The cast of *The Four Men* during the 2017 tour of the play, adapted for stage by Ann Feloy. The production was performed by Conn Artists Theatre Company, www. conn-artists.co.uk.

The Battleground

POLITICS, POLITICIANS, AND REVOLUTION.

Better remain silent, better not even think, if you are not prepared to act.
ANNIE BESANT

Imagine the scene: a general election is taking place, perhaps the most important general election for a generation. The Liberals are hoping to take power from the Conservatives, who have been in government for all but two of the last twenty years. One seat the Liberals have to win if they hope to form the new administration is Salford South. Their candidate is a thirty-five year old Anglo-French journalist and author, only recently naturalised as a British citizen. If he is to win he needs to play down his foreignness, and that includes his adherence to the Roman Catholic religion. His political advisers, including his agent, stress this point: there are many non-conformists in the constituency, who are in no mood to vote for a French Catholic. The day arrives for the first public meeting. The year is 1905, a time when election meetings were public spectacles and a form of raucous, popular entertainment: the hall is packed with a loud and fractious mob. The Liberal candidate gets up to speak:

> Gentlemen, I am a Catholic. As far as possible, I go to Mass every day. This [taking a rosary out of his pocket] is rosary. As far as possible, I kneel down and tell these beads every day. If you reject me on account of my religion, I shall thank God that he has spared me the indignity of being your representative.[1]

1   Speaight, Robert, The *Life of Hilaire Belloc* (Hollis & Carter 1957), p. 204

Hushed silence, followed by extended cheering. This was Hilaire Belloc's entry into the world of politics. Having stunned the hall, he then continued to tell the audience who he was and what he stood for: "This man is no foreigner, but an Englishman who talks a Radicalism which is not talked in any other country but England."[2]

In order to 'spice up the election,' it is said that Belloc paid local boys to chalk up the following graffiti on walls around the constituency:

A Frenchman there was named Hilaire
And Rene – the names make you stare;
He wished to be a Salford M.P.
But they wanted no foreigners there.[3]

Belloc's electoral strategy appears to have been to rouse his opponents in order to face them down, to make it appear that they were motivated by personal dislike and guile, while he was interested in policies and changing people's lives for the better. If it was his strategy, it certainly worked, and Belloc was elected with a substantial majority. On election night, amidst the cheers of his supporters, he was going to Westminster:

On a whole-hearted and well-defined democratic programme, such as that on which Mr John Burns was returned for Battersea twelve years ago. Liberalism of that kind will spread. It is like lighting a fire that you cannot put out. They cannot put me out of Parliament till Parliament is dissolved, and before that time comes, I intend to let the people at St. Stephen's [Green – where parliament stands] hear a few truths in the interests of the working classes that will astonish them.[4]

Before considering Belloc's time in parliament, we should go back to 1889, and look at the great event of that year that shaped Belloc's political outlook. This was the year of the Great London Dock Strike, a strike for better wages, that gave birth to militant trade unionism in this country, and a strike (as we have seen), that was tacitly supported by Cardinal

2   *Ibid*, p. 206
3   *Ibid*
4   *Ibid*

Manning, the Catholic Archbishop of Westminster. The leaders of the strike became famous in their own right, one, John Burns, went onto to be a Liberal MP, another, Ben Tillett, went onto to be one of the most well-known and militant trade union leaders in the country. For a time, the strike leaders were gaoled, and many feared a repeat of the riots of two years earlier, when the poor of the East-end rampaged through the fashionable thoroughfares of Mayfair and Belgravia. Revolution seemed to be in the air, as Belloc recalled in later life:

> Well do I remember the fevers of that struggle! I was but nineteen years of age; it was my delight to follow the intense passions of the time; and those passions were real. It was before the socialist creed had been captured for the sham battle at Westminster. The leaders did desire, and did think they could achieve an England in which the poor should be poor no longer, and in which there should be sustenance and happiness for all....I remember the great mobs that followed John Burns, and how I myself would go miles through the East End to hear him; and I remember that great whirlpool of men in Trafalgar Square on the most critical day when he and others accepted imprisonment.[5]

The phrase "before the socialist creed had been captured for the sham battle at Westminster," should alert us to the interpretation the older Belloc gave to the experience of his younger self.

Belloc as a young man was full of indignation about the impact that industrial capitalism was having on ordinary people, he was also outraged by the dispossessions of small farmers and the loss of common rights that had been enjoyed for centuries:

> Within the memory of people still living a sufficient number of Englishmen were owning (as small free-holders, small masters, etc.) to give to the institution of property coupled with freedom a very vivid effect upon the popular mind. More than this, there was a living tradition proceeding from the lips of men who could still bear living testimony to the relics of a better state of things. I have spoken when I was a boy to old men in the

---

5   *Ibid*, pp. 44 – 45

neighbourhood of Oxford, who had risked their skins in armed protest against the enclosure of certain commons, and who had, of course, suffered imprisonment by a wealthy judge as the reward of their courage; and I have myself spoken in Lancashire to old men who could retrace for me, either from personal experience the last phases of small ownership in the textile trade, or, from what their fathers had told me, the conditions of a time when small and well-divided ownership in cottage looms was actually common.[6]

Here again, we should notice the emphasis that Belloc gives to ownership and therefore his longing to see property, not abolished (as the communists demanded), but rather its restoration to the great mass of people. It is the injustice of property being concentrated in a few hands, not the concept of property itself that Belloc objects to; in his poem 'The Justice of the Peace', he lays bare the cruel reality of a world where a few wealthy men owned the land:

Distinguish carefully between these two,
This thing is yours, that other thing is mine.
You have a shirt, a brimless hat, a shoe
And half a coat. I am the Lord benign
Of fifty hundred acres of fat land
To which I have a right. You understand?

I have a right because I have, because,
Because I have – because I have a right.
Now be quite calm and good, obey the laws,
Remember your low station, do not fight
Against the goad, because you know, it pricks
Whenever the uncleanly demos kicks.

I do not envy you your hat, your shoe.
Why should you envy me my small estate?
It's fearfully illogical in you
To fight with economic force and fate.

6   *Ibid* p. 318

Moreover, I have got the upper hand,
And I mean to keep it. Do you understand?[7]

Belloc lived through an era where newspapers were proving an ever more important tool of social control. An ever more literate population had access to new ideas which might not incline them to support the current political and social system. William Cobbett's *Political Register* had galvanised political radicals across England in the early nineteenth century, just as Robert Blatchford's, *The Clarion*, did in Belloc's early adulthood. Clearly the masses needed to be provided with an antidote to these dangerous ideas and men of wealth and power ensured that such newspapers were brought into existence. It is surely no coincidence, that both the *Daily Mail* and the *Daily Express* were launched at the very moment the English working class was being moved an influenced by ideas of social change and social justice?

Belloc saw very clearly that the purpose of the 'popular press' was to stem the tide of change and divert their readers attention towards trivia and gossip:

> ... the press of our great cities is controlled by a very few men, whose object is not the discussion of public affairs, still less the giving of full information to their fellow-citizens, but the piling up of private fortune. As these men are not, as a rule, educated men, nor particularly concerned with the fortunes of the State, nor capable of understanding from the past what the future may be, they will never take up a great movement until it is forced upon them ... they will waste energy in getting up false excitement upon insignificant matters.[8]

In the 1920s, Belloc noted that there would never be a free stream of information in England until we "Dam the Beaverbrook and Dredge the Rothermere," a reference to the two lords who owned most of the country's newspapers.

---

7   Wilson, A.N. (Ed), *Hilaire Belloc, Complete Verse* (Pimlico 1991), p. 147
8   Speaight, *ibid*, pp. 151 – 152

As his life, including his political life, took many twists and turns, he remained consistent in his belief in the 'redistribution' as opposed to the monopoly or the abolition of property. It was a view that sat uncomfortably with either the socialist or the capitalist point of view, and as a result, Belloc can appear at one moment a revolutionary, and at another, a reactionary. This uneasy, we could say, untenable position, born from his sense of what a Christian, Catholic society should be like, forced him to make political choices in later life that have besmirched his reputation among subsequent generations.

Even as late as 1927, Belloc was still forcefully expressing the views he had held since the Great Dock Strike of nearly 40 years earlier, although now with an even greater sense of urgency:

> The industrial civilisation which, thank God, oppresses only the small part of the world in which we are most inextricably bound up, will break down and therefore end from its monstrous wickedness, folly, ineptitude, leading to a restoration of sane, ordinary human affairs.... based as a whole upon the freedom of the citizens. Or it will break down and lead to nothing but a desert. Or it will lead the mass of men to become contended slaves, with a few rich men controlling them. Take your choice.[9]

Belloc always saw history as a way of understanding the present, rather than as an act of nostalgia or an intellectual exercise for academics: what could the past tell us and how could it help us understand our current predicament and forge a better future? These were the questions that fascinated him. He wrote many dozens of historical books. Some of his later ones were little more than rehashed versions of earlier ones, all conveying the same message – late medieval society was Reformation, and its bastard child, capitalism.

Rather like the great Victorian historian, Thomas Carlyle, Belloc believed that "History is an imprisoned Epic," which "illuminates the dark ways of God."[10] Like, Carlyle, his fundamentally reactionary position

9   Boyle, David, *Back to the Land, Distributism and the politics of life* (The Real Press 2019), pp. 65 – 66.
10 Rosenberg, John, D, *Carlyle and the Burden of History* (Harvard University Press 1985), p. 160

regarding the Reformation and the emergence of capitalism could also concede the need for revolution when all other options had failed, or where no other option was available. Belloc believed that the French Revolution of 1789 had been necessary: "otherwise society would have withered up." Or as Carlyle put it, "We will hail the French Revolution, as ship-wrecked mariners might the sternest rock, in a world otherwise all of baseless seas and waves."[11]

However, The French Revolution, gave birth to nationalism, an ideology that Belloc identified as dangerous, as it was "a force destructive of the unity"[12] of Europe. It was also in competition with, rather than complimentary to Catholicism, something to be deplored.

It was his writing of English history, rather than French, that caused the ire of his countrymen. A people brought up on the idea of empire and the good influence of this country on world affairs, were not going to take kindly to being told that their most cherished historical canards, were no more than myths, and dangerous myths at that. Here is Belloc taking a great swipe at the 'Golden Age' of Queen Elizabeth and her trusty 'English seadogs,' such as Drake and Raleigh:

> It is true that a race of bold seaman arose contemporaneously with the reign, but they were no more remarkable than the captains of other nations in Europe at the same time and they nearly all bore the taint of theft and murder. They were slave-dealers and pirates, secretly supported by the powerful men of the State; Elizabeth could not but feel the shame which their piracies brought upon her in the eyes of her fellow sovereigns, and yet could not avoid taking part in the proceeds of the disgraceful business.[13]

In recent years, the novels of Hilary Mantel have become extraordinarily popular in this country, especially her trilogy about Henry VIII's fixer-in-chief, Thomas Cromwell. It is interesting that Mantel should have sought to make such a man the subject for her fiction and that she chose to paint him in such a favourable light. For Belloc, Cromwell was a man without

11 *Ibid*, p. 96
12 Speaight, *Ibid*, p. 132
13 Belloc, Hilaire, *Characters of the Reformation* (Sheed and Ward 1936), p. 171

honour or belief, a shifty and ruthless operative, motivated by money and power.

One is certainly struck by the contrasting ways that Mantel and Belloc describe Cromwell's end. In Mantel's version we are presented with a man stoic and pragmatic in the face of death; indeed his death is not depicted at all, rather we see him walk to the scaffold as if entering a holy light of heavenly absorption. Nothing in Mantel's version about the desperate pleas Cromwell made for his own life, or the botched beheading by a drunken executioner, that saw the wretched man's neck cut apart in chunks. Even England's 'greatest living novelist' (who sadly died just a few days before this chapter was written) felt obliged to side with myth rather than fact. Belloc had no such qualms:

> He was condemned to death by attainder without trail and made the few
> days between the condemnation and his death both pitiable and memorable
> by the imploring letters he wrote the King begging and even screaming for
> life. He ended one with the famous cry, 'Mercy! Mercy! Mercy!' He fawned
> and cringed, using the most extraordinary phrases, comparing Henry to
> God and saying that the perfume of the royal hand would waft him to
> Heaven if he were allowed to kiss it again.[14]

Belloc claimed that as a man of no religion, Cromwell was terrified of death, but at the very last he repented and accepted the true faith (Catholicism). Where this was the case or not, Belloc had no doubt as to Cromwell's legacy:

> But his work was accomplished before his head fell; he had effected the
> breach with Rome, and by his loot of the Church he had made possible all
> the further steps by which England was transformed to a Protestant country
> from a Catholic country, at the same time giving the whole governing class
> of England a strong financial motive for never allowing the Mass to return
> to England if they could help it.[15]

14 *Ibid*, pp. 95 – 96
15 *Ibid*, p. 96 – 97

That 'financial motive,' being of course the Dissolution of the Monasteries and the sale of church lands, by Cromwell and the King, to the wealthy men of England at a knock-down price, from which even greater wealth was produced. Yet it is the Mantel version, even in 2022 that we prefer to hear – Cromwell the clever, insightful administrator, who steered England away from superstition and ignorance to an age of enlightenment and prosperity. So great and enduring are national myths.

An Unsuccessful Politician

Belloc was not a successful politician. He was not a team player nor was he a 'party man.' As we have seen, he lived for the big picture; one moment gazing back to the past, the next straining his eyes to discern dim outlines on the horizon of the future. Yet, politics is the business of the here and now, the art, as Harold Wilson said, "of the possible." For Belloc what was possible was that which needed to be done, but as that would involve, of necessity, overturning nearly four hundred years of national history, that was hardly likely to be very possible at all.

Belloc did not sit easily on the government benches. He alienated far more than he persuaded. Men used to positions 'on the right', 'on the left,' or 'in the centre,' of British politics, could hardly understand a man who seemed to jump effortlessly between all three positons.

Over the next five years, Belloc took up many causes, very few of which endeared him to his colleagues. He opposed attempts to restrict the drinking of alcohol, including the Local Veto Bill: "Opportunity has little to do with drunkenness. Drunkenness is due to the desire for getting drunk".[16] He opposed equal voting rights for women with men and this would "disrupt the balance between the sexes".[17] He supported Home Rule for Ireland and famously raised the case of the editor of an Irish Nationalist newspaper, who had been dragged out of his offices by police in a snow storm. Pointing to the Conservative benches, he wondered how honoura-

---

16 Speaight, *Life of Hilaire Belloc, ibid*, p. 87
17 Speaight, *Life of Hilaire Belloc, ibid*, p. 280. For a fuller explanation of Belloc's attitude towards female suffrage, see Pearce, ibid, pp. 134 – 136.

ble members would take to being dragged out of the Carlton Club in a snow storm, but, of course, such an occurrence was unthinkable!

He opposed Anglicanism being taught exclusively in state schools and successfully campaigned for state funding for Catholic and other denominational schools. He opposed attempts to 'criminalise the poor,' and spent hours on the floor of the House of Commons opposing the Infinite Sentencing Bill, that would have allowed judges to imprison men indefinitely, successfully, restricting the maximum sentence that could be passed for a non-mandatory sentence (e.g. murder, arson etc.), to five years – "may God reward me for it,"[18] he exclaimed afterwards.

He greatly disliked attempts to 'reform the working class' and to limit or close down popular entertainments or pastimes. He was particularly outraged that the police could arrest a man for singing in the street if this was judged a breach of the peace, and that a vagrant could be arrested for begging and arrested for wandering with the intention of begging. Belloc was more interested in tackling the causes of an unfair society rather than its symptoms.

As the 1910 election approached, he admitted that the prospect did not fill him with joy:

> I am very dejected about the approaching election. I don't want to stand. I detest the vulgar futility of the whole business and the grave risks to which are attached no proportionate reward. So anxious are most people to get into Parliament that they will do anything to oust an opponent, and I have really no desire to be mixed up with such hatreds, or see myself placarded on the walls in twenty ridiculous attitudes, and with any number of false statements or suggestions attached to my name. It is a perfectly beastly trade.[19]

Fighting elections was not without personal risk in those days. Edward Turnour, Earl Winterton, had been elected at the same time as Belloc, indeed Winterton's constituency included Belloc's home at Shipley. Winterton recalled the elections in those early days: "Candidates and their agents were assaulted, heads and windows were broken, usually without

18 Speaight, *ibid*, p. 231
19 Speaight *ibid*, p. 240

any prosecution following. It was considered to be the point of the game – the inalienable right of the Briton to be rowdy and lawless on certain recognised occasions."[20]

Yet, Belloc put his doubts to one side. The Liberal government had promised to introduce Old Age Pensions, but this and other aspects of Lloyd George's 'People's Budget' were being blocked by the House of Lords. Then there was still the unresolved matter of Irish Home Rule. Belloc felt he had to go back into the fray in the hope that the election would break the deadlock on these issues. Indeed, as the campaigned progressed, Belloc regained something of his old enthusiasm:

> England is at a turning-point. Society is trembling with the desire to produce a new and better England. But it cannot be done without raising great sums of money and without putting burdens on the rich. If it is going to be done at all, it is going to be done in the next few weeks. An old man said to me the other day, 'This is the first election I remember in which something is going to happen.' That is true. You are either going to push the great weight of social reform and democracy over the edge and send it down the other side, or you are going to allow it to slip back on yourselves and crush you.[21]

He also hoped that "all those who have the right to call themselves democrats desire Englishmen to sit round one table and be brothers."[22]

Robert Speaight has left us a very evocative, even graphic account of that election in January 1910:

> Belloc and his wife drove around in an open carriage. Some threw mud at them and others cheered. Even the children of Salford [got involved in the tumult]. One little Tory of tender years ran after the carriage shouting, 'Tear him oop! Tear him oop!'; whereupon a lifelong Liberal of about the same age called out from a doorway, 'Ah'll stick thee in the bahels!'. These were politics and this was Lancashire. Polling day was January 15. While the count was being taken Belloc amused himself – and perhaps others – by

20 Winterton, Earl, *Fifty Tumultous Years* (Hutchinson), pp. 123 – 124
21 Speaight, *ibid*, p. 280
22 *Ibid*, p. 282

ragging his opponent …. The result was declared on placards posted on the upper windows of the Town Hall in Bexley Square; below, the crowd waited in a downpour and blew tin trumpets. When it was known that Belloc was just in by 314 votes, red lights were burned in a neighbouring street, and Irishwomen in the crowd mobbed and kissed him as he reached the Exchange Club with victory in his eyes and practically no voice.[23]

Nationally, the result of the election was deadlock, with the Conservatives and Liberals evenly matched and the Labour Party and Irish Nationalists holding the balance. The scene was set for stalemate and deadlock. The months dragged on and then, at the height of the crisis – with the Liberal government threatening to create hundreds of Liberal peers to flood the House of Lords and thereby push through their proposals – King Edward VII died.

Belloc attended the King's funeral. He enjoyed the pomp, although not the sentimental aspects of the occasion:

> … a most impressive sight marred by not a few bits of detestable music-hall business the worst of which was the King's dog [paraded along with the cortege]. The Queen Mother went on just as though she was on the stage, which was very unpleasant to see.[24]

Belloc was also disappointed that few of the assembled monarchs from other countries could ride horses, "but the young King of Portugal could."[25]

This account is suggestive of a depressive mood descending on Belloc coupled with a restlessness that the stalemate in the House of Commons did not improve. As Belloc sat on his bench in the chamber, he looked from one side to the other, and wondered just how real the contest was. Here were a collection of rich men, many of whom were related, and nearly all of whom had more in common with each other than the people who had elected them. He was weary, very weary of the whole business. When Prime Minister H.H. Asquith called a snap election for December

23 *Ibid*, p. 283
24 *Ibid*, p. 286
25 *Ibid*, p. 286

1910, in another attempt to break the deadlock, Belloc knew he could not be a part of it:

> I can't believe the Grocers and Pawnbrokers who control the caucus in Salford will stand a candidate pledged to ridicule and criticize the Party System, and if they won't have me independent they shan't have me at all: if they will have me they will be idiots, for I shall be defeated and they will have paid for nothing.[26]

In his letter to 'the caucus,' he was more kindly, "I wish to reassert, in closing this letter, my very great esteem and regard for and gratitude towards, those who have financially supported my candidature and the other expenses of my organisation."[27] But, grateful or not, Belloc was bowing out of Parliament and party politics.

One socialist in his constituency, pleaded with Belloc to change his mind, telling him: "your courage, your outspoken desire for straight politics and your advocacy of the democratic ideal have not gone unregarded in this land". Belloc graciously replied, thanking the men for his kind words, but assuring him that his mind was made up:

> Moreover one must be inside the House of Commons to see how utterly futile is any attempt at representative action. It is all very well as advertisement, but it is without ant practical consequence whatever, and it is like trying to feed on air to attempt to satisfy the appetite for action under such conditions. I agree with you that realities may enter politics soon, and when they do, I shall re-enter politics with them ….[28]

Belloc never re-entered politics.

Like a great love affair suddenly ended, the sense of loss and bitterness set in over the following months and years. At a meeting of the Permanent Protest League in Worthing on 2nd February 1912, Belloc thundered that he was glad to be quit from "the vilest and dirtiest"[29] company it had ever

---

26 *Ibid*, p. 293
27 Speaight, Robert, *Letters From Hilaire Belloc* (Hollis & Carter 1958), p. 19
28 Speaight, *Life of Hilaire Belloc*, p. 293
29 *Worthing Mercury*, 3rd February 1912, p. 5

been his misfortune to keep. More than this, he also spoke out against some of the proposals of the Liberal government, that only just over a year ago, he was still representing in the House of Commons. He singled out the National Insurance Bill for special criticism. He did not think it was the business of the government to take money from men's wages in order to cover them in time of sickness: 'It's like the State saying – Belloc, we notice that your boots are in a disreputable condition. In future you will pay £1 a year to the State, and the State will find you in boots!"[30]

One correspondent, writing to a Worthing newspaper the following week had not been impressed by Belloc's performance in the town, and preferred instead to quote former Conservative Prime Minister, Arthur Balfour:

> ... Mr Balfour has frequently spoken in terms of praise of the House of Commons, and reasonable people will prefer to take his view rather than that of Mr Belloc, who has a poor case; hence his abuse of the House which still prefers the company of gentlemen.[31]

It was Arthur Balfour, who famously commented, when pressed on what were the great issues of the day that "nothing matters very much and few things matters at all."[32] For Belloc, nearly everything mattered, and a few things mattered more than most, especially the truth.

Later in 1912, Belloc collaborated with the journalist, Cecil Chesterton, to expose corruption in high places, indeed corruption in the heart of government. In the pages of the *New Witness*, they showed how government ministers had profited by buying shares in the Marconi Company, when they knew that this company was about to be awarded a highly lucrative contract to provide His Majesty's Government with exclusive wireless radio technology.

Those named and implicated were, Godfrey de Bouillon Isaacs, Managing Director of the Marconi Company, Herbert Samuel, the Postmaster General (and future Liberal leader), Sir Rufus Isaacs, the

---

30 *Ibid*
31 *Worthing Mercury,* 10th February 1912
32 Wikiquotes

Attorney General (and later Lord Chief Justice), and David Lloyd George (later Prime Minister).

There had been no scandal like it in British politics for over one hundred years. Belloc held his ground as the storm broke around him. When he had left the House of Commons for the last time in December 1910, Lloyd George had made a point of going over to Belloc and saying how sorry he was that he was leaving, "Ah!" said Belloc, "but I, like my Saviour, will rise again on the Third Day," which he noted, "shocked that little Welsh Nonconformist."[33]

Where Belloc stuck to the facts, Cecil Chesterton pushed on, making further, unsubstantiated allegations. What is worse, he shrouded them in anti-Semitic rhetoric, with the result he was successfully convicted of criminal libel. In the House of Commons, Lloyd George and Herbert Samuel expressed their regret for any indiscretion they may have unwittingly committed and the matter was allowed to drop.

Belloc was furious with Cecil Chesterton for allowing his passions to get the better of him and shift attention from the guilty men, but he was more furious that all sides in the House Commons seemed more interested in protecting their own than in exposing the truth. At this time Belloc was on very friendly terms with the Conservative politician, George Wyndham, who was related to the Earls of Leconfield and Egremont, heirs to the Petworth estate in West Sussex. The two men, despite their very different backgrounds, found they had much in common, and would go for long walks together, discussing, politics, religion and the mortality of the soul. When Wyndham died suddenly in 1913, aged only 49, Belloc was devastated.

We may wonder if Belloc's friendship with Wyndham and his frustration with what we might today call the 'Nanny State' point of view, gave rise to his comic verse of 'Lord Rumbo and Lord Jumbo':

Lord Rumbo was a Democrat
Who wore a very curious hat
And woollen boots, and didn't think
It right to smoke or take a drink.

33 Wilson, A.N., *Hilaire Belloc* (Hamish Hamilton 1984), p. 174

He also thought it rather wrong
To hum the chorus of a song.
But what he simply couldn't stand
Was Billiard Tables off the Strand!

Yes, Billiard Tables off the Strand!
Lord Jumbo, on the other hand,
Was quite another sort of cove,
What? Yes by God! – and also Jove.[34]

He was a Tory thick and thin.
His hat was made of Beaver Skin.
He practised every kind of sport
And drank a dreadful deal of Port.

After the Revolution

Belloc was deeply involved with sustaining and supporting the British cause during the First World War, but as his attitude towards war is considered in chapter six, we will not discuss it here. Rather, we will consider his response to the Russian Revolution of 1917, and specifically, his reaction to the Bolshevik coup, known to history as the 'October Revolution.'

Although Belloc was no friend of the rich and powerful, and had cut his political teeth following and supporting the striking dockers in 1889, it would be a mistake to believe he ever considered himself a socialist. Belloc, as we have seen, was calling for the greater distribution, not the abolition of property. This simple truth may not have been apparent to those on the Left, who saw him as a natural ally. Yet his position regarding state intervention in the life of the individual had already been made apparent in his opposition to the National Insurance Bill. Even as a young man, before he entered parliament, he had made his position very clear in regards to state socialism:

34 Wilson, A.N. (Ed), *Complete Verse, ibid*, p. 215

How could collectivisation work, without a military despotism? How could it work with the existing attitude of the individual conscience unchanged? In fact, it involves Theft in its inception, and Tyranny in its execution, and for neither in Society yet ready.[35]

The Russian Revolution needs to be understood in its two distinct phases: the first phase saw a general rebellion across society against the incompetence of the Tsarist government, and especially against its conduct of the war, that had led to many privations, as well as many casualties. Peasant conscripts were at the forefront of the uprising. During the spring and summer of 1917, liberal political parties sought to bring about reform while continuing to pursue the war and since the mass of soldiers and sailors wanted the war to end, this was a policy doomed to fail. The Bolshevik party (later renamed the Communist Party) exploited this grievance to their advantage and under the pretence of giving 'all power to the soviets' (the worker-led factory committees), used their organizational and military superiority to forcibly wrest control from the provisional government.

Planned elections to a national assembly, or Duma, were allowed to take place. In these elections, the Bolsheviks were decisively defeated by the Social Revolutionary Party. Faced with this inconvenient reality, Lenin, the Bolshevik leader, sent armed Bolsheviks (later to be coalesced as the 'Red Army') to close down the Duma, thus ending Russia's very brief experiment with parliamentary democracy.

The Bolshevik Revolution was a cause of hope and much rejoicing among revolutionary socialists the world over, who saw the dramatic events in Russia as the culmination of all their hopes and struggles. However, there were important exceptions. In the United States, Ralph Chaplin, one of the leaders of the International Workers of the World, and the man who had written their stirring anthem, 'Solidarity for Ever!' soon turned against the Bolsheviks. He became aware that many non-Bolshevik revolutionaries in Russia were being arrested, tortured and 'disappearing.' Peter Kropotkin, the revered Russian anarchist denounced the tyranny of the Bolsheviks.

35 Speaight, *ibid*, p. 88

In Britain, Robert Blatchford, the man who had done more than most to popularise socialist ideas in this country, was alarmed by the stories of repression coming out of Russia, and listened with growing concern to the warnings that Kropotkin and others were giving about the Bolsheviks and their motives. Blatchford would later say that if this was socialism, then he and other members of his 'Clarion Fellowship' had never been socialists, as they had always believed that socialism would liberate and free humankind, not suppress and enslave it.

Lastly, we should let the Bolsheviks speak for themselves. In his book, *The State and Revolution*, Lenin had set out the route by which the communists would seize and retain power, a process that would involve the dictatorship of the working class as envisioned by 'their' revolutionary party. It was left to Leon Trotsky, the founder of the Red Army, to set out in stark terms what living under this revolutionary state would mean in practice:

> Coercion, regimentation, and militarization of labour were no mere emergency measures and the workers state normally had the right to coerce any citizen to perform any work at any place of its choosing.[36]

This historical background to the Bolshevik coup and the reaction of other socialists to the new revolutionary government gives context to Belloc's response and suggest that he was not alone in his deep unease about what had happened and what would continue to unfold in Russia.

Writing in 1922, by which time the Bolsheviks had defeated all their enemies in Russia, and established one-party rule, Belloc sought to show how their revolution differed from previous examples:

> The Revolutions of the past were for the better distribution of property and for the betterment of the State. Often they were openly undertaken because patriotism had been offended by defeat in war and because the Nation was thought to be betrayed. Usually they were jingo [nationalistic] and always for distribution of wealth.[37]

---

36 Deutscher, Isaac, The Prophet Armed (Oxford Paperbacks 1970), p. 500
37 Belloc, Hilaire, The Jews (Constable & Co 1928)), p. 171

What had happened in Russia was different:

> It is the unique mark of the Russian revolution and its attempted extension elsewhere that it repudiates patriotism and the division of property.[38]

Belloc did not believe the frequent claims in the British Press that the Bolsheviks 'were on their last legs,' but asserted that the government in Moscow "has taken root, and is firmly established." He also believed that "though they reign by terror, they reign also by an appeal to popular instincts and indignations which are very strong," adding, "the Russian peasant believes that through them he has acquired his lands."

Belloc also believed that it was very significant that most of the Bolshevik leadership was Jewish – the Jews having suffered relentless persecution under the Tsarist regime. It was not, therefore, surprising to find them at the forefront of the revolution. It was contentions such as this that have led to accusations of anti-Semitism against Belloc, accusations that are dealt with in a subsequent chapter in this book.

In 1922, Belloc could not have foreseen the forced 'collectivisation' of the peasantry in the late 1920s, that far from allowing them to "acquire" there lands, once again reduced them to a form of serfdom and servitude. Many hundreds of thousands, possibly even millions, died in the famine that followed, most in the Ukraine.

As 'copycat' revolutions broke out across Europe, often being suppressed with great brutality, Belloc perceived how essential it was to the government in Moscow that these insurrections in other countries should continue:

> Communism must be international if it is to succeed. A Communist society may stand apart from the general society of owners in other countries, but if it is to succeed in competition with them it must convert them to its own creed.[39]

As socialist movements across the world converted themselves into

---

38 *Ibid*
39 *Ibid*, p. 175

communist parties, so the danger of the horrors seen in Russia being replicating in other countries became ever more likely. Moscow united these parties into a Communist International. Georgi Dimitrov, the General Secretary of the 'International' suggested how communists could best spread their revolution to other countries:

> Comrades, you will remember the ancient tale of the capture of Troy. The attacking army was unable to achieve victory until, with the aid of the Trojan Horse, it penetrated to the very heart of the enemy camp. We, revolutionary workers, should not be shy of using the same tactics.[40]

In the US, Ralph Chaplin spent most of his waking hours exposing and opposing the communist infiltration of the trade unions in his country. In Britain, Robert Blatchford, urged his supporters to do the unthinkable, and vote Conservative, as the only sure way to oppose the threat of communism. Even Aneurin Bevan, for ever revered in British socialist circles as the founder of the National Health Service, told his comrades to resist the allure of communism: "Its relationship to democratic institutions is that of the death watch beetle", he warned, "it is not a Party, it is a conspiracy."[41]

Fascism

It was against this backdrop of violence and the threat of violence across the world, that Belloc, was led into what one of his biographers, Joseph Pearce, has called 'treacherous waters.'[42] Belloc could have no sympathy with Lenin or Trotsky, but neither could he reconcile himself with the capitalist system, so he was going to be attracted to a 'third way' between these two unpalatable options.

In France, Belloc was attracted to the fiery rhetoric of Charles Murras, whose Action Francaise advocated a return to strong government based

40 Corrin, Jay P., 'Hilaire Belloc and the Spanish Civil War' in *The Chesterton Review*, May 1986, p. 205
41 Quoted in 'Scorn', by Matthew Parris (Profile Books 2016), p. 102
42 Pearce, Joseph, *Old Thunder, A Life of Hilaire Belloc* (Harper Collins 2002), p. 195

on social justice and French traditions and values. In Italy, the fascist movement not only advocated similar themes of autocratic benevolence, they actually brought them to fruition, by seizing power in their 'March on Rome' in 1922. Many who feared the dictatorship of communism now welcomed the dictatorship of fascism, among them Hilaire Belloc. In 1924, he travelled to Rome to meet Benito Mussolini and was spellbound:

> I had the honour of a long conversation with him alone, discovering and receiving his judgements. What a contrast with the sly and shifty talk of your parliamentarian! What a sense of decision, of sincerity, of serving the nation and of serving it towards a known end with a definite will! Meeting this man after talking to the parliamentarians in other countries was like meeting with some athletic friend of one's boyhood after an afternoon with racing touts; or it was like coming upon good wine in a Pyrenean village after compulsory draughts of marsh water in the mosses of the moors above, during some long day's travels over the range.[43]

It is hard not to flinch from such unfettered praise. Even allowing for the benefit of hindsight and our knowledge of what evils fascism represented, it is still unseemly to find a man in his mid-fifties, gushing with such adolescent hero-worship. Belloc detested hero-worship, yet here he is indulging in it; worse still, he was endorsing a political approach entirely at odds with everything he had been arguing for over the previous 35 years, as Pearce has highlighted:

> Enshrined within Belloc's distributism, and at the very heart of the Church's social teaching which had been Belloc's inspiration, was the principle of subsidiarity. This stipulated that political and economic power should begin with the family and that the usurpation of such power by big business or central government should be rectified by its devolution from larger to smaller institutions. Such a creed was essentially libertarian and did not sit comfortably with political dictatorship. Yet Belloc's desire for a 'Europe of the Faith' led him to support Mussolini in Italy and Maurras in France on the somewhat naïve assumption, at least with the benefit of

---

43 Wilson, Hilaire Belloc, *ibid*, p. 290

hindsight, that their strong anti-capitalist and anti-communist stance would result in the resurrection of Catholic Europe. Significantly, he chose to ignore the fact that neither Mussolini nor Maurras were practising Catholics.[44]

It was actually far worse than them not being practising Catholics. Mussolini was an ardent atheist. He had once dared God to strike him dead for disbelieving in him, and declared, "The Bible and morals called Christian are two cadavers [corpses]."[45] All this should have been obvious to Belloc with his deep knowledge of classical antiquity. He should have recalled how the Roman emperors saw themselves as gods. Mussolini consciously modelled himself and his movement on Imperial Rome. Belloc had no excuse, except the excuse of wanting to believe in something better than the evils of capitalism and communism he had already committed himself to opposing.

Belloc in the 1920s and '30s is a man simultaneously following two contradictory paths. Only as the 1930s draw to a close, does he come close to resolving these contradictions. In 1926, while Mussolini is rounding up his opponents and supressing independent trade unions, Belloc is supporting the General Strike in England. More than that, he is bemoaning the failure of those with wealth to support the poor in their hour of need:

> We are in a state of permanent and sullen civil war, modified by general patriotism and terror of the police and troopers. The rich are seeing to it that these divisions shall grow more acute. God has blinded them. I have not met one single gentleman or lady on the side of the poor in this crisis. That's ominous.[46]

More than this, Belloc attacked the entire economic system that Britain had imposed on much of the world, although he believed that Britain's lead in world affairs was passing to the United States, for whom he argued, a new generation were being schooled to regard as the bastion of the

44 Pearce, *ibid*, p. 195
45 Found in quotepark.com
46 *Ibid*, p. 227

98

values Britain have stood for and revered for centuries. At the same time, the poor in England and in its overseas territories were being condemned and blamed for resenting the system that ruthlessly exploited them; yet, he argued, such hubristic pride could not endure indefinitely:

> We survive to-day to hear a perpetual flattering of America, a perpetual grumbling against the workers, their sullenness, and overseas, the increasing peril of control over the alien races once so easily governed. The vulgarians who invented this music-hall cry of empire now suffer the vacillation and the increasing peril into which their own base bullying have led them. They must live a little time longer and dree their weird, and learn what happens to those forms of pride which have not even the merit of dignity.[47]

They must "dree their weird": an eerily archaic verdict passed on the ruling classes by a man whose mind was as present in pagan antiquity as it was in 1920s Britain. Belloc could readily see the imminent collapse of Britain as a world power and the crumbling of its empire, when nearly everyone else seemed blind to such an eventuality. He also recognised, long before it seems to have occurred to other commentators, that Britain was already a second class power, and that the country's political leadership had connived in this usurpation: "Had they known a plain, modern historical truth, that America is a foreign country," he wrote, "they could have preserved an independent national policy. It is now too late. America has mastered us."[48]

Belloc still railed against industrial capitalism: "the monstrous state of affairs in which a very few men derive their vast advantage from the corresponding fact that most men whom they exploit do not own."[49] In his poem, 'The Garden Party,' he ridiculed the insidious class system that kept everyone in England strictly in their place. Even those elements of privilege, such as duty and tradition that may have had something to commend them, were wilting under the eroding torrent of modern capitalism and the corresponding moral decline:

47 Belloc, Hilaire, *The Cruise of the Nona* (Constable & Co 1955), p. 235
48 *Ibid*, pp. 139 – 140
49 Belloc, *The Jews, ibid*, p. 173

The Rich arrived in pairs
And also in Rolls Royces;
They talked of their affairs
In loud and strident voices.

(The Husbands and the Wives
Of this select society
Lead independent lives
Of infinite variety.)

The Poor arrived in Fords,
Whose features they resembled;
They laughed to see so many Lords
And Ladies all assembled.

The People in Between
Looked underdone and harassed
And out of place and mean,
And horribly embarrassed.

For the hoary social curse
Gets hoarier and hoarier,
And stinks a trifle worse
Than in the days of Queen Victoria,
When they married and gave in marriage,
They danced at the County Ball,
And some of them kept a carriage.
And the flood destroyed them all.[50]

Belloc continued to support 'Musso' in Italy, writing with glee: "Every day Mussolini's policy and actions appear in a better light – he seems to make no mistakes and our politicians look sillier and sillier." He believed that Italians liked to see the rich in their country subordinated to the rule of The Duce, and that in Italy at least, the excesses of capitalism had been tamed.

---

50 Wilson, A.N. (Ed), Complete Verse, *ibid*, p. 219

The Spanish Civil War

In 1936 the Spanish Civil War broke out, occasioned by the attempt of conservative generals, supported by The Falange, the Spanish fascist movement, to overthrow the elected socialist government. The general who soon emerged as the leader of this rebellion, Franco, began the war with atrocities, and continued to use this method throughout the conflict. The fascist troops sent by Mussolini to support Franco, were ruthless in the extreme, but even they were shocked when told to shoot children of Republicans captured in the fighting. Yet Belloc described Franco as "the man who has saved us all," and likened him to General Foch, the French Commander of the Allied Forces in the Great War.

It should be remembered that even among those who went from Britain to Spain to fight fascism, many came back with stories of how the peoples' revolution had been subverted and taken over by the communists. This story of betrayal was most vividly recounted in George Orwell's *Homage to Catalonia.*

Belloc visited Spain during the civil war. He knew the country well and was deeply affected by Spanish culture. He met and had an interview with General Moscardo, whose brutal ruthlessness was legendary. On capturing Alcazar, Moscardo not only ordered the execution of all captured male fighters, but 20 pregnant women found in the hospital, were also reportedly murdered. If ever evil stalked a land in human form, it was Moscardo. After meeting General Franco himself, the man ultimately responsible for all this carnage, Belloc indulged in the fantasy of believing he had met 'Roland of the Marches,' one of his French medieval heroes, reborn. Belloc was smitten: "God had blinded him" to an even greater degree than the lords and ladies whom he had condemned for turning their faces away from the suffering of the poor in England ten years earlier during the General Strike.

Belloc did not want to hear about the evil of fascism in Spain. He did not believe it. These were lies put around by the enemy, an enemy at war not just with civilisation, but with Christianity itself. It was the stories of massacres committed by communists and anarchists that Belloc chose to believe in. He would have read with horror about the reports of the bodies of nuns and monks being dug up and hung from lampposts, or otherwise exposed to public gaze and mockery. Ernest Hemingway, who fought with the Republicans in the Civil War and was therefore no friend of the Catholic Church, described seeing a captured priest scrambling for his life as revolutionaries tore him open with "sickles and reaping hooks,"[51] and that his heinous screams did nothing to dim the ardour of their murderous rampage.

Belloc's entire belief system was based on his Catholic faith, and on the sanctity of holy places and objects, and the reverence due to all places of burial. It is not hard to understand why Belloc took the stance he did, but that cannot excuse him. Not only was he in the wrong morally, he was also in the wrong historically, which given the great significance he attached to history and the lessons it could teach, is indeed a severe judgement. Once Franco died, his system of suppression fell apart. Spain, more than any other country in Europe embraced the permissive society in all its guises.

This writer, visiting Spain as a seventeen year-old in 1979, was astonished at how explicit pornography was freely available on every newsstand – and this only four years after the death of the dictator. Until recently, Spain had the lowest age of consent in Europe. Frozen in time for 36 years, Spain rejected Franco and all he stood for when given the opportunity. As Belloc grudgingly admitted in 1938, as he began to see Mussolini in the cold light of day, "tyranny cannot be sustained indefinitely." Franco ruled through fear, not through love and what is Christianity without love?

It was Mussolini's introduction of anti-Jewish laws in 1938 that turned Belloc against the fascist leader. However, his attitude had already been shifting. Mussolini's invasion of the ancient Christian kingdom of Abyssinia in 1935 left Belloc in a position where he was unable to justify the aggression: "What I regret is the possible disappearance of an old native kingdom. The end of anything ancient is always to be deplored unless it were the Devil."[52]

---

51 Hemingway, Ernest, For Whom the Bell Tolls (Granada Publishing, 1976), pp. 116 – 117
52 Speaight, *ibid,* p. 435

The Nazis

Belloc's dalliance with fascism was drawn to a close by the rise of its German counterpart: Nazism. To begin with, Belloc did not see the danger in Adolf Hitler, convinced as he was, by the existential threat of communism. He was convinced that Hitler was no more than a puppet of the German General Staff, a means by which they could reassert their old power and dominance. In 1932, on visiting Germany, he observed that the Nazi election campaign "was no more exciting than the sheep fair at Findon."[53] He would soon change his tune.

By 1936, he was writing that Christianity in Germany was "disappearing rapidly from the German mind,"[54] and that it was being replaced by a new a sinister belief:

> They have a religion, as indeed all men must have a religion, for men cannot live without something to worship. That religion is the worship of the German race as the highest thing on earth, and of what we can only translate as Germanism as the supreme German good.[55]

In Germany itself, the Nazi leaders were making very clear that Christianity would have no place in the Thousand Year Reich. Martin Bormann declared, "National Socialism and Christianity are irreconcilable."[56] Hitler himself stated: "One day we want to be in a position where only complete idiots stand in the pulpit to preach to old women."[57] Meanwhile, Himmler was busy erecting statues to Germanic pagan deities and building up his library of witchcraft.

By 1939, not only was Belloc fully aware of the absolute need to defeat Nazism, he also realised how its rise had been aided by the great financial institutions, who had lent the Nazi regime loans on favourable terms: "This German monstrosity was brought into being by the Bank of England

---

53 Speaight, *Letters to Hilaire Belloc, ibid,* letter to Duff Cooper, p. 227
54 Pearce, *ibid,* p. 254
55 *Ibid,* pp. 254 – 255
56 Hughes, Matthew, and Mann, Chris, *Inside Hitler's Germany, Life Under the Third Reich* (Brown Reference Group 2004), p. 80
57 *Ibid.*

under the orders of which our politicians also helped build up the new Germany, and now we must take the consequence."[58]

Belloc believed that British politicians and civil servants could have created an alliance with France against Germany, but had chosen not to do so because their racial sympathies were with Germany. To be fair to Belloc, it was Mussolini who had first reacted against Hitler, mobilising his forces against the man he denounced as a barbarian. By 1938, Mussolini had become little more than an appendage to Hitler, adopting the Nazi-style racial laws.

We may agree with Robert Speaight, that Belloc in the early 1930s, was unable to fully grasp the magnitude of the evil that was arising in Europe, even though he himself had long predicted its emergence: "[He] was too civilized and reasonable a man, too steeped in the Latin tradition, to imagine the power of paranoia raised to the pitch of maleficent genius. His incapacity to sympathise with mysticism made it impossible for him to appreciate its parody."[59]

We will consider Belloc's position regarding the Second World War in chapter six. It must be remembered that after the stroke he suffered on 30th January 1942, Belloc played no further part in the politics of his country. Writing in 1953, the year of his death, Reneé Haynes, in her assessment of Belloc's political life, reminded her readers that Belloc, was, first and foremost, an opponent of modern capitalism, something that his misguided dalliance with fascism had obscured:

> As the vast structure of industrial capitalism changes, crumbles or collapses, it may be recollected that Belloc saw and detested as vividly as any Marxist its vast injustices and its advertising-slogan self-justifications; and that he put forward a remedy conceived in terms of constructive human happiness instead of one based upon the misery of mechanized mass-revolution.[60]

Belloc also warned that society was most vulnerable when the middle class

---

58 Pearce, *ibid*, p. 261
59 Speaight, *Life of Hilaire Belloc, ibid*, p. 435
60 Haynes, Reneé, *Hilaire Belloc, Writers and their Work*, No. 35 (Longmans, Green & Co. 1953), p. 29

of society "weakens or is destroyed."[61] This nearly happened in England and other European countries in the early nineteenth century, leading to widespread revolution; although in England, the ruling class relented, and absorbed the wealthier ranks of the middle class into the governing elite. Belloc believed that the creating of a class chasm between rich and poor had led to the collapse of ancient pagan civilisation. "The more the disease of Industrial Capitalism develops,"[62] he wrote, the more likely that such a disaster could be visited on our own civilisation. This warning – like so many Belloc issued in the 1920s and '30s – may seem both timely and relevant to our own times?

61 Belloc, Hilaire, *An Essay on the Restoration of Property* (Distributist Books 1936), pp 78 – 79
62 *Ibid.*

'The Greatest anti-Semite of the Twentieth Century'

BELLOC THE BIGOT, OR BELLOC THE CRITICAL FRIEND?

But for my part, I say, "Peace be to Israel."
HILAIRE BELLOC

Listening to Radio 4 sometime in the early to mid-1980s, this writer was rather startled to hear the late Greville Janner MP (later Lord Braunstone) describe Hilaire Belloc as "the greatest anti-Semite of the twentieth century." Presumably, he added "in Britain," but it is only that bald and shocking statement that stays in the mind. Readers may recall that Mr Janner himself was the subject to some pretty unsavoury allegations towards the end of his life; but it is his allegation against Belloc that concerns us here. Was Belloc a bigot and a racist? There are many who think so. In her review of Richard Ingrams' 2021 book, *The Sins of G K Chesterton,* in the *Times Saturday Review*, Melanie McDonagh asserted that Chesterton had adopted anti-Semitic ideas due to the malign influence that Hilaire Belloc had over him in this regard[1]. In a review of the same book in *The Spectator*, Duncan Wu asserted that Chesterton had adopted "the anti-Semitic views of Hilaire Belloc, to whom Jews were un-British parasites, consisting largely of bankers and businessmen determined to take over the world."[2]

Let us then consider the evidence for the prosecution. In doing so, you are asked to read to the end of the chapter before making up your mind as

1   *The Times* Saturday Review, 14th August 2021
2   *The Spectator*, 21st August 2021

to whether Belloc was indeed the Jew-hating bigot that he is frequently described as being. The media has great power and influence, but that does not automatically mean they are right or that we should believe what they say.

Edward Turnour (later Baron Turnour) was Conservative MP for Horsham from 1904 until 1951 and had the distinction of being the youngest member (21) when first elected, and later, the longest serving member (Father of the House) from 1945 – 1951. Belloc, as we have seen, was not well suited to parliamentary life, and served only five years as an MP. Turnour (known to his constituents as Winterton, as he was heir to an Irish earldom of that name), knew Belloc well. They were both young MPs together and Winterton was Belloc's constituency MP for all but the last two years of Belloc's life at Shipley. Belloc gets a mention in Winterton's two-volume autobiography, published after Winterton had retired from the House. The reference is almost entirely taken up with Belloc's conduct towards a Jewish member:

[Belloc] was a prominent and brilliant participant in Union debates in his Oxford days. He made one or two good speeches [in the House of Commons] and then committed a fatal error. The late Mr Harry Lawson (afterwards Lord Burnham), a popular and much respected man, had just concluded a mild and unprovocative speech from our benches when Mr Belloc rose and, in his rather high-pitched voice, began, "In extended observation of the Anglo-Judaic plutocracy I...." He got no further. This obvious reference to Mr Lawson was received with angry cries from the Conservative benches of "order, withdraw, cad!!", whilst his Liberal colleagues sat in silent disapproval, which is always a sure sign that a member has made a grievous mistake. Neither in the rest of the speech nor in any others that he subsequently made did he recover from this mistake. The House of Commons did not approve of him for all his talents and fine qualities which I, as a friend of his, appreciate. Nor, to judge from subsequent reference to politicians in his writings, did he approve of the House of Commons.[3]

3   Winterton, Edward Turnour, *Orders of the Day* (Cassell & Company 1953), p. 45

None of Belloc's biographers refer to this speech, nor to Harry Lawson and Belloc's attitude towards him; yet we must assume Winterton didn't make it up nor the hostile reaction that the speech received. Whether, after 50 years, he accurately remembered what had taken place, or the gravity of it, is open to speculation. Having stepped down from the House in December 1910, Belloc wrote of his despair of 'the Party System', but that he was "glad Winterton represents me in Parliament and Sussex is itself again."[4] That is the only reference I have been able to find of Winterton in Belloc's writings. There is no evidence of personal hostility between the two men that could lead us to doubt Winterton's account, although whether the two men were actually friends, as Winterton suggests, may be more doubtful.

Belloc did not like the fact that many Jewish families, such as the Lawsons, had adopted anglicised surnames. He felt this was underhand and deceptive. His full sarcasm on this account is very apparent in the verse he wrote following the death of Lord Swaythling, the former Liberal MP and prominent banker:

> Lord Swaythling whom we loved and knew
> On earth as Mr Montagu,
> Will probably be known in hell
> As Mr Moses Samuel:
> For though they do not sound the same,
> The latter was his real name.[5]

A.N. Wilson believes that a hostility towards Jews was nurtured within Belloc during the time he was serving as a young man in the French Army. France was a country with a far greater history of anti-Semitism than Britain, and nowhere was this more apparent than in the country's military, as evidenced by the Dreyfus scandal with all its dire implications for France, its armed forces, and its sense of national identity. Writing not long after his return to England from France, the young Belloc was fired

4   Speaight, Robert, *Letters from Hilaire Belloc* (Hollis & Carter 1958), letter to Maurice Baring, p. 29
5   Wilson, A.N., *Hilaire Belloc* (Hamish Hamilton 1984), pp. 173 – 174

up with the political radicalism that would lead him into parliament, and great indignation against the financial and banking system. He wrote of his sympathy with the 'Red Republicans' and their desire for a more just society: a day that was surely coming, when, "the whole round world will be as happy as in the old times before the Jew came to the land."

Those sour words were written by a young man, who would eventually change his position politically, so should we not be prepared to believe he could change his position on the Jews as well? The evidence of his writings from his middle years suggest he was not a man with hatred in his heart for the Jewish people, although the ideas and prejudices of his youth came back to haunt Belloc in old age, when he was suffering with dementia. In 1946, when the full horrors of the Nazi crimes against the Jews of Europe were being revealed, Belloc, in his dotage at Shipley, was asked by a visitor what he thought about recent events. "I am not an anti-Semite," Belloc explained, "I love 'em, poor dears. Get on very well with them. Poor darlings – it must be terrible to be born with the knowledge that you belong to the enemies of the human race." When asked to explain his last statement, he simply replied, "The Crucifixion."[6] This is Belloc evoking his sense of 'weird' and the consequences of actions. He was not a well man in 1946 and his mental powers were considerably dimmed. It may be wondered to what extent, if at all, he grasped the enormity of the concentration camps and their appalling legacy.

I would argue that Belloc's perceived hostility towards Jews was primarily a hostility towards the banking and financial system generally, in which Jews were disproportionately represented. When attacking this system, he had no compunction in singling out the particular characteristics of wealthy men, be they cultural or racial, by which to mock or undermine them. This is not a method most political adversaries would choose to deploy today, and a good thing too; but Belloc was not writing in our times or with our sensibilities. His verse on Lord Rothschild's imposing house in London is typical of the comic verse he deployed to ridicule adversaries:

---

6   Pearce, Joseph, *Old Thunder, A Life of Hilaire Belloc* (Harper Collins 2002), p. 276

At the end of Piccadilly is a place
Of habitation for the Jewish race.
Awaiting their regained Jerusalem.
These little huts, they say, suffice for them.
Here Rothschild lives, chief of the tribe abhorr'd
Who tried to put to death Our Blessed Lord.
But, on the third day, as the Gospel Shows,
Cheating their machinations, He arose:
In whose commemoration, now and then,
We persecute these curly-headed men.[7]

Not a pleasant read. A.N. Wilson, who quotes it in his book on Belloc, references it as 'Oral Tradition,' and supplies no more information; so it is conceivable Belloc never spoke these lines, or if he did, the 'Chinese whispers' of oral tradition has embellished them. In his published comic verse, Belloc let aim at all the English ruling class, whatever their origins. The idiot Lord Lundy, who had been singled out at birth to be "the next Prime Minster but three" but greatly disappointed his grandfather, who dispatched him to "govern New South Wales." Belloc is always seeking to puncture pomposity and expose privilege and entitlement. "Lord Lucky" only becomes a duke due to the untimely death of all the other possible contenders. The hero of that poem is 'Mr Meyer,' for whom we are invited to feel sympathy. Meyer is not a Rothschild, but a modest man.[8] Belloc disliked political corruption and he disliked pomposity, so when the two were combined, he was liable to make his displeasure known in verse:

The grocer Hudson, he
When purchasing his barony
Considered, as we understand,
The title of Lord Sugarsand,

7   Wilson, *ibid*, p. 258
8   Wilson, A.N., *Hilaire Belloc, Complete Verse* (Pimlico 1991), pp. 213 – 214, the lines: "But after his succession/ though all this was years ago/ He only once indulged the whim/ of asking Meyer to lunch with him," suggests Belloc's empathy for Jews being excluded from certain circles of 'polite society.'

Or then again he could have been
Lord Underweight of Margarine,
But, being of the nobler sort,
He took the name of Devonport.[9]

Belloc was not an ideological racist; in fact he rather deplored the concept of race. He disliked Darwin and his theories and rigorously dismissed any idea of 'the ascent of man,' or the existence of superior races. It is doubtful if Hitler or Mussolini would have enjoyed this lampooning ditty:

Behold, my child, the Nordic Man
And be like him as you can.
His legs are long; his mind is slow;
His hair is lank and made of tow.

And here we have the Alpine Race.
Oh! What a broad and foolish face!
His skin is of a dirty yellow,
He is a most unpleasant fellow.

The most degraded of them all
Mediterranean we call;
His hair is crisp, and even curls,
And he is saucy with the girls.[10]

This is outrageousness for its own sake. It is not to be taken seriously. Belloc blustered and boomed, especially if he was harassed, tired and not enjoying himself. In these moods his excessive language, including cultural stereotyping, was all too apparent, as in this exasperated letter he sent to G.K. Chesterton from Venice:

Venice! The ceaseless whisper of the tout; the threat of backsheash upon all sides: the insolent hangers-on; the sly Jews; the pickpockets: the incredible prices of simple things: the absence of dignity. Venice![11]

9   *Ibid*, p. 232
10 Wilson, *Complete Verse, ibid*, p. 221
11 Speaight, *Letters, ibid*, letter to G.K.Chesterton, p. 93

In his great public campaigns, and in his book on the Jews, Belloc refrained from outrage for outrage's sake and actually chose his words carefully and with considered purpose. This side of the man deserves as much, if not more attention, than the irreverent and naughty schoolboy of the comic verses.

In chapter three, we saw how Belloc was deeply involved in exposing the Marconi scandal in 1912 through his articles in the *New Witness* newspaper. The editor was Cecil Chesterton, the younger brother of G.K. Chesterton. J.B. Morton believed that Cecil Chesterton hugely influenced Belloc, even though he was younger and less well-read:

> It is possible that [Belloc] overrated Cecil Chesterton. Cecil was not a deeply educated man. A brilliant debater and a superb stylist, resolute in action and intrepid in controversy, he was too thoroughly a journalist in the literal sense of feeling and thinking from day to day to give at all times a balanced judgement on the complicated problems of an ancient and subtle society. He had immense virtues of which the chief were loyalty, candour and courage; these endeared him to Belloc ....[12]

As we have seen, several of the chief protagonists in the Marconi scandal were Jewish, although the most prominent of all, the Chancellor of the Exchequer, David Lloyd George, was Welsh. As the scandal broadened and the pressure on Chesterton as editor grew, so he increasingly lashed out at Jews in positions of power in Britain; worse still, he printed virulently anti-Jewish articles by Hugh O'Donnell, a journalist whose instincts were feral. Godfrey Isaacs, the managing director of the Marconi company and brother of the Attorney General, Rufus Isaacs, sued Chesterton for criminal libel, a prosecution that brought with it the likelihood of a custodial sentence if proven. Writing to a friend in February 1913, Belloc agreed that the articles in the *New Witness* were "hitting blind" and not addressing the real issue of insider trading and government corruption:

> For instance, the detestation of the Jewish cosmopolitan influence, especially through finance, is one thing, and one may be right or wrong in feeling that

12 Morton, J.B., *A Memoir of Hilaire Belloc* (Hollis and Carter 1955), pp. 297 – 298

112

detestation or in the degree to which one admits it; but mere anti-Semitism and a mere attack on a Jew because he is a Jew is quite another matter, and I told him repeatedly that I thought the things he allowed O'Donnell to publish were unwise and deplorable ....[13]

He continued:

... Englishmen naturally suspect exaggeration ... when, therefore, an opponent can be pointed at as quite irrational about something, and as having brought in utterly extraneous matter it does him more harm in England than anywhere else. This is just what O'Donnell's letters have done and many other passages unsigned in which the national term 'Jew' has been used simply as a term of abuse, much as lower middle-class Americans will use the term 'Irish.'

In a further letter, written a few weeks later, Belloc returned to his theme:

The irritation against Jewish power in Western Europe is partly friction between the two races, but much more the annoyance of feeling that non-national financial power can restrict our information and affect our lives in all sorts of ways....But just because these matters so nearly verge upon violent emotion, it is essential to avoid anything like the suspicion of fanaticism. It destroys all one's case and weakens all one's efforts ....[14]

Robert Speaight has a very clear insight into Belloc's state of mind at this time. Having given up his political career, he could have returned to writing history, especially his well-received French histories, but that was not to be:

The friendship of Cecil Chesterton cost Belloc several years of embittering controversy. Such controversy, with its technique of direct personal attack, is dangerous for the soul ... If you dislike Mr Lloyd George or Sir Alfred Mond as much as Belloc disliked them, it is better not to think about them too much. But Belloc thought about them incessantly. This is what his

13 Speaight, *Life of Hilaire Belloc, ibid*, p. 311
14 *Ibid*, 363

admirers mean when they say that Cecil Chesterton was bad for him. They are thinking of another *Danton* or *Marie Antoinette*, a better *History of England*, that he might have written if he had been content to sit quietly at King's Land. But the answer is that, with or without Cecil Chesterton, he would never have sat quietly at King's Land. To sit quietly anywhere, he would have had to be quite a different sort of man.[15]

Sir Alfred Mond was one of the great industrialists of his day. As chairman of ICI in 1928, Mond entered into an agreement with Ben Turner, the General Secretary of the TUC, whereby all future negotiations regarding pay and conditions would be conducted through officially recognised trade unions. To Belloc this reeked of a stitch-up, whereby the workers conceded the right of ownership to the capitalists, while the workers transferred their bargaining rights to the union. It should be said that, to many people at the time, this just seemed like a good old English compromise, and far preferable to the revolution and civil war brewing across much of Europe.

What is interesting about this event and Speaight's singling out of Mond as a man Belloc thoroughly disliked, is that it did not stop Belloc sharing an air raid shelter with him during a German bombing raid in the Great War, nor did it stop Mond offering, and Belloc accepting, a Cuban cigar – "the only Cuban cigar I ever liked."[16] Apart from Rothschild, no one represented 'the Jewish power' in Britain more absolutely than Alfred Mond (later created Lord Melchett), yet Belloc expressed no personal animosity towards him. This is why he disapproved of Cecil Chesterton's attacks – they were so emotional: Belloc was motivated by ideas and the promotion of ideas that were good and the rejection of ideas that were bad. Whether he was right or wrong in his appraisal of a good idea is another matter, but the intense personal rancour that is implicit in racist attitudes was not something Belloc really understood; perhaps if he had understood them he would have been more careful on occasion how he expressed himself in matters of race and religion.

15 Speaight, *Life of Hilaire Belloc, ibid*, p. 299
16 Speaight, Letters, *ibid*, letter to Duff Cooper, p. 212

The turmoil of the First World War, concluding as it did with revolutions across much of Europe, including the successful Bolshevik seizure of power in Russia, greatly fuelled anti-Semitism, not just in Europe, but also in the United States. During the 1920s, the Ku Klux Klan held huge rallies, not only in the Southern states, but also in New York. The notorious Tsarist secret police forgery, *The Protocols of the Elders of Zion*, which purported to prove the existence of a world-wide Jewish conspiracy, was widely read and widely believed. In Germany, Hitler wrote *Mein Kampf*, while serving a prison sentence for his part in an abortive coup. Everywhere, it seemed, there was the threat of revolution and counter revolution.

Into this febrile atmosphere, Belloc published, in 1922, his book, *The Jews*, with a second edition with a new preface being published six years later. Even the title of the book is enough to put a modern reader on high alert – 'The Jews' – doesn't this of itself suggest an accusation? Why write such a book at such a time of heightened passions if not to inflame them? Belloc dedicated the book to his Jewish secretary:

To
Miss Ruby Goldsmith
My Secretary for many years at King's
Land and the best and most intimate of
Our Jewish friends, to whom my
Family and I will always owe
A deep debt of gratitude[17]

Belloc states that his purpose in writing the book is to avert a catastrophe that he saw looming for the Jewish people due to their close association, in the public mind, with international finance on one hand, and atheistic, revolutionary communism on the other. Belloc did not stint in stating the danger to which he believed this public mind-set could lead: "In the legitimate anger against a few pitiful dozens among the worst specimens

---

17   Belloc, Hilaire, *The Jews* (Constable and Co. 1928), p. v

of the nation, Israel as a whole will be sacrificed."[18] Furthermore, he believed that the pogroms that the Jews of Poland and Russia had suffered at the beginning of the century could be nothing compared to what they might suffer in the future: "The last state of the Jews in Eastern Europe will be worse than the first."[19] The blaming of Jews for the excesses of both capitalism and socialism could have dire consequences: "It will perhaps prove the immediate cause of that explosion against the Jews which we all dread and which the best of us, I hope are trying to avert."[20]

Writing in *The Tablet* in July 2020 – the 150th anniversary of Belloc's birth, A.N. Wilson, while highlighting many of Belloc's qualities, felt compelled to condemn him for his anti-Semitism, writing: "I have never found a scintilla of evidence that Belloc could see a connection between the sort of anti-Semitic views he expressed throughout his life and the horrors of the Third Reich."[21] If this is what one of Belloc's biographers believes, how can any defence of Belloc on this issue possibly be maintained? Yet, surely, Belloc was clearly warning of the terrible dangers the Jews of Europe faced 11 years before the Nazis came to power and 20 years before the start of the mass killings in the concentration camps?

Let us look more closely at what Belloc was writing about the Jews and ideas of world conspiracies in the 1920s. Was he fudging the matter or was he clearly endorsing or condemning the idea of an international Jewish conspiracy – the very idea that sustained the Nazis in Germany and the Klan in America?

In *The Jews*, he sets out the historical relationship between the Jews in Europe and the native populations of individual European countries. He recounts the tragic cycle of Jews becoming successful in commercial life and often indispensable in political life, only then to face extreme and violent backlashes – to find themselves blamed for economic and military defeats that were not of their making. In Britain, Belloc charts the close relationship between certain Sephardic Jewish families and the British

---

18 *Ibid*, p. 93
19 *Ibid*, p. 90
20 *Ibid*, p. 91
21 *The Tablet*, 25th July 2020

State and how this close relationship helped create and perpetuate the British Empire: "the interests of international Jewish finance and of British Commerce were for a long time nearly identical."[22] He notes the leading role of Jews in British diplomacy and espionage.[23]

No country in Europe was more sympathetic than England to Jewish interests and more willing to sympathise with the persecution they had suffered in other countries:

> The English were not only Protestant, their middle class were steeped in the reading of the Old Testament. The Jews seemed to them heroes of an epic and the shrines of a religion. You will find strong relics of this attitude in Provincial England to this day. One should add a certain national distaste for violence, which feeling was exasperated by hearing of Jewish persecution abroad. One should also further add the pride which modern Englishmen take in feeling that their country is an asylum for the oppressed.[24]

Reneé Haynes, in her monograph on Belloc, makes an interesting point here, one that concerns theological adherence to the Old Testament rather than the New, something that both Jews and 'Bible Christians' had in common. Belloc preferred to see the spiritual connection of Christian revelation to pagan antiquity, rather than to the Judaic law of pre-Christian scripture. Belloc, Haynes has suggested, saw Judaism and Protestantism "harking back" to "the primitively apprehended idea of God in the Old Testament, [which] seemed to regard financial success as the earnest of divine approval, and to replace love and contemplation as the mainspring of living by work and money-making."[25] Whether this is actually what Belloc thought or how Belloc would have expressed it, we can't tell, but it is an observation that is not out of keeping with all we know about Belloc and his perception of the world.

---

22 *Ibid*, p. 205
23 Britain's most famous early twentieth century spy, Zigmund Rozenblum, AKA, Sidney Reilly, 'Ace of Spies' is a case in point.
24 Belloc, *The Jews, Ibid*, p. 221
25 Haynes, Reneé, *Hilaire Belloc, Writers and their Work*, No. 35 (Longmans, Green & Co 1953), p. 18

In regards to the Russian Revolution, Belloc was not surprised that most of the leaders of the Bolshevik Party were Jewish – no group had suffered more at the hands of the Tsarist state than the Jews. They were also an educated people and they were an international people – they were not confined to one national territory. Belloc believed that it was this combination of factors that explained the leading role of Jews in revolutionary movements. Not being sentimentally attached to the nations they were living in, they were more likely to grasp and appreciate concepts and ideas that eschewed national boundaries, be that capitalism or socialism, so it was no paradox to find Jews in both camps: "Now the attack on this international phenomenon, an attack directed against Industrial Capitalism, required an international force. It needed men who had international experience and were ready with an international formula."[26]

Belloc is forensic in his analysis, but he never descends into hyperbole or zealotry. As for the idea of the revolution in Russia being part of an international Jewish conspiracy, involving the entire ethnic group, he dismisses the notion out of hand:

> Thus we are asked to believe that this political upheaval was part of one highly-organised plot, centuries old, the agents of which were millions of human beings all pledged to the destruction of our society and acting in complete discipline under a few leaders superhumanly wise! The thing is nonsense on the face of it. Men have no capacity for acting in this fashion. They are far too limited, far too diverse….the conception of a vast age-long plot, culminating in the contemporary Russian affair, will not hold water.[27]

Belloc argued for an understanding between Jews and non-Jews that would allow each side to better appreciate the other's point of view. He could see the merit in a Jewish homeland, but that should not be at the expense of existing Arab populations. If such a homeland were created, it would not be right for powerful Jewish interests to maintain economic

26 Belloc, *The Jews, ibid,* p. 172
27 *Ibid,* pp. 168 – 169

and political power in other countries. This argument, made in the 1920s, was done so at a time of far greater cultural homogeneity than exists today: most modern Jews, for example are secular rather than religious; the same being true of most European peoples. Yet, the archaic presumption aside, there is no doubting the sincerity of Belloc's desire for harmony between Jews and non-Jews:

> I am convinced that if we on our side get rid of this absurd modern fear, take the Jew in his right proportions, rid our mind of exaggeration in his regard – especially of the conception of some inhuman ability capable of conducting a plot of diabolical ingenuity and magnitude – we shall be met from the other side.[28]

Belloc warned of the danger to the Jewish people of finding a too powerful protector. It had been Britain, in the future it might be another great power: "No great nation will sacrifice its foreign policy, will admit a point of acute weakness simply to please the Jews. Sooner or later such a nation is bound to say: 'we cannot sacrifice our interests to yours. Look after yourselves.' And that is where the peril to the Jews of this system ... comes in."[29]

Belloc did not foresee a United States of the future giving exactly this protection to the state of Israel, but does his warning still hold true? Belloc was aware of the degraded state of the Arab populations in the Middle East. He noted that the Jews in Algeria could vote, while the Arab Muslims could not. He observed that, historically, Jews had suffered less oppression under Islam than they had in Christian countries, but that situation was changing due to the Arab perception that the West favoured Jewish interests over their own. Where, he wondered, would this end? It would be very foolish if the West ignored 'the flaming spirit of Islam,' assuming it was a fire that could be quenched or tamed.

It is interesting to note that Theodr Herzl, the founder of modern Zionism, was very aware of making a pitch to Western interests in his appeal for the creation of a Jewish state in Palestine: "We should there

28 *Ibid*, p. 267
29 *Ibid*, p. 221

form a portion of the rampart of Europe against Asia, an outpost of civilisation as opposed to barbarism."[30] Is this not exactly how the USA regards the Israeli state today? The relationship between America and Israel appears impregnable, but history has a nasty habit of taking sudden and unexpected turns. Belloc's warning still holds true.

In 1923, the year after the publication of his book, Belloc visited America and Canada where he was faced with anti-Semitism in the raw. He had not encountered such a mood before, not even in the days of his youth in the French Army, as he explained in a letter sent to a friend back in England:

> Those who know I have written a book on [the Jews] take it for granted that I am in approval of a general massacre – which is the usual extreme confusion Americans reach when they have worked themselves up on the matter, while the very much smaller number who have actually read my book, disagree with its judicial tone: they want blood and thunder. But much the greater part of those I hear talking have no idea I have written about it – and all in Toronto, Buffalo, New York, Pittsburg, Boston, everywhere rave and howl against the Jews. It may or may not come to [a violent] outbreak – on the whole I think not – but it makes the life of the mass of Jews here – who are poor – very hard. Magistrates are....biased against them – they are insulted in public and refused entry to clubs and even hotels and in general made to feel like they are enemies – what a life! Fancy some wretched man coming with his family from, say, Poland, and landing into this! For the American has no tradition or habit in the matter and never appreciates complexity. He feels the racial friction and reacts in the shape of violent revulsion.[31]

Belloc was indeed shocked. When he considered all he saw and heard, coupled with the recent history of America: its colonisation of the West, its intervention in Latin American countries, its increasingly lawless and gang infested cities, he concluded, "the Americans yield to none in

---

30 Gilbert, Martin, *From the Ends of the Earth, The Jews in the Twentieth Century* (Cassell 2001) p.22
31 Speaight, *Life of Hilaire Belloc, ibid*, pp.454 – 455

promiscuous violence and bloodletting."[32] If Belloc's book received a lukewarm reception, there was another book selling in large numbers, *The Cause of the World Unrest* (published anonymously and wrongly attributed to Nata Helen Webster), in which the writer blamed all the ills of the world on malign Jewish influence. People in America wrote to Belloc about Webster's work and he responded in a forthright manner:

> In my opinion it is a lunatic book. She [Webster] is one of those people who have got one cause on the brain. It is the good old Jewish revolutionary bogey. I think people are great fools who do not appreciate what part the Jew has played in revolutionary movements, but people are much bigger fools who get it on the brain and ascribe every revolutionary movement to Jews and secret societies. The prime cause of revolution is injustice, and the protest against injustice, when it becomes violent, produces revolution. But there is a type of unstable mind which cannot rest without morbid imaginings, and the conception of single causes simplifies thought. With this good woman it is the Jews, with some people it is the Jesuits, with others Freemasons and so on. The world is more complex than that. Many of the facts quoted are true enough, but the inferences drawn are exaggerated. It is perfectly true that the Jews were the leaders and remain the leaders of the Russian Revolution, but there was much more in it than that.[33]

By the time that the second edition of Belloc's Jewish book was published, Trotsky had been forced into exile and the Georgian former trainee-priest, Stalin, had assumed power in the Soviet Union. Over the following years, Stalin purged the entire Bolshevik leadership, including its Jewish members, most of whom he had executed. Only a 'great fool' indeed would have considered Communist Russia a 'Jewish tool' following the show trials of the 1930s. During the Second World War, Stalin appealed to Russian patriotic spirit and the Russian Orthodox Church to bring him victory over Hitler. Even with victory achieved, Stalin continued to purge

---

32 Wilson, A.N., *Hilaire Belloc* (Hamish Hamilton 1984), p.345
33 Speaight, *Life of Belloc, ibid*, pp.456 – 457

and oppress Jews in Russia, despite the invaluable contribution many had made towards the war effort.

Back in England, Belloc found that few in the Jewish community were persuaded by, or appreciative of, his book, including those Jews he judged to be his friends:

> A Jewish adviser – one Benjamin – whom I trusted to judge wisely and to whom I submitted the proofs – has said the book is unjust and that his people will refuse to read it or sell it, etc. It saddens me: for if the Jews don't accept a just solution in time they are doomed to a renewal of misery. I have put the case as justly as I could.[34]

To Ruby Goldsmith (to whom he had dedicated the book), he wrote:

> I am rather afraid the Jews attack me because apparently one thing they cannot bear is a work seriously dealing with their problem. They do not seem to mind being violently abused nearly so much as a severe analysis of the situation. I regret this. I think that the security and happiness of the Jewish community in the future depends almost entirely upon their facing the facts. Nearly every one I know has got Jewish friends – that proves that the differences between the two races need not lead to hatred or bitterness.[35]

Again, we have the (to us) archaic and offensive assumption of cultural homogeneity and common ethnic ideology. It is also not hard to see why a Jewish person, especially one who was educated and successful in business, should not react well to being told about 'solutions' to 'their problem.' Yet, equally, we can see that Belloc was hurt and even bewildered by the rebukes he received. If the Jews did 'attack' him (presumably a reference to articles in the national press at the time) it did not make him bitter or cause him to intensify his rhetoric or narrow his point of view. In the preface to the second edition of *The Jews*, he made an appeal for tolerance, understanding and friendship:

> When the book first appeared it was called by those who had not read it 'Anti-Semitic' – that is, a book written in antagonism to Jews by a man who

34 Speaight, Letters, *ibid,* letter to Mrs Reginald Balfour, p. 116
35 Wilson, *Hilaire Belloc, ibid,* p. 272

hated Jews. I have no antagonism of this kind. So far from hating the Jewish people, I seek their company, I enjoy their conversation, and of my friends the proportion who are either wholly or partly of Jewish blood is large .... National and racial hatreds are common enough. We are all weary of the hatred of the Irish, which has done incalculable harm to this country; and I hope we are becoming equally weary of the contempt, if not hatred, for the other nations belonging to the Catholic culture of Europe. Crude hostility of this sort solves nothing, and I shall never descend to it. Every mundane thing is good in its right place, and evil in its wrong place. May Israel have peace.[36]

Belloc, after all, was an outsider himself. He had empathy for the Jewish situation for it was not unlike his own in many respects. He too thought more internationally than nationally, and he valued intelligence and ancient learning far more than the ephemeral and fleeting slogans of politicians or the screaming headlines in the popular press.

The reader may judge for themselves whether the late Greville Janner was right in his contention that Belloc was "the greatest anti-Semite of the twentieth century," or agree with A.N. Wilson that there was a connection between Belloc's writings and the outpouring of hatred directed against the Jews of Europe by the German Nazis.

36 Belloc, *The Jews, ibid,* preface to 1928 edition, pp. xv – xvi

To Fight or Not to Fight?

FROM BOERS TO HITLER.

The brazen throat of war had ceast to roar.

JOHN MILTON

Rather like his attitude towards the Jewish people, Belloc's attitude towards war often seemed conflicted. Clearly, the circumstances of each conflict affected his judgement – not all wars can be judged by the same yardstick; but there was more to it than that: Belloc felt keenly the suffering that war brought in its wake, even if he supported the cause that underpinned it.

The same young man who had uttered anti-Semitic remarks also gloried in the prospect of a European war, "How I long for war," he enthused, "It will sweep Europe like a broom, it will make Kings jump like coffee beans on a roaster."[1] We must give some slack to a nineteen year-old impatient for change to come to a continent that seemed to be stultified by autocracy and privilege; we should also bear in mind, as with his Jewish comments, they are made distasteful to the modern reader who has the benefit of hindsight – the knowledge of knowing what carnage and cruelty two world wars delivered.

Shortly after writing these words, Belloc served his time in the French Army, which, as we have seen, deeply influenced his view of the world and shaped his ideas regarding men and their motives. The men with whom he served in the artillery came from varied backgrounds and were of very different personality types:

> My Captain was a man promoted from the ranks; one of my lieutenants was an Alsatian Charity boy and the other a rich fellow mixed up with sugar; the

1   Speaight, Robert, *The Life of Hilaire Belloc* (Hollis & Carter 1957), p.41

124

sergeant of my piece was a poor young noble, the wheeler of No. 5 a wealthy and very vulgar chemist's son, the man in the next bed a cook of some skill and my bombardier a mild young farmer.[2]

When, a few years later, Belloc went to read history at Balliol College, Oxford, he alone among his fellow-students could claim to have lived, breathed and laboured with men of all classes (as well as having travelled the length of America); it was what made him (along with his Catholicism), such an exotic and unique personality among the young gentlemen from Eton and Harrow.

Another thing that the French Army taught him was how to adapt to difficult circumstances, including the vagaries of rough and ready soldiery. It also brought him the joy of learning and singing old French Army songs, songs that contained in them:

A whole expression of the barrack-room; its extreme coarseness; its steady and perpetual humour; its hatred of the hard conditions of discipline; and also these songs continually portray the distant but delightful picture of things – I mean of things rare and far-off – which must ever lie at the back of men's minds when they have much work to do with their hands and much living in the open air.[3]

Belloc learned that 20 years earlier, his battery had lost every one of its commissioned and non-commissioned officers during the war with Prussia.[4] There can be no doubt that this knowledge left Belloc with an abiding antipathy towards German military intentions and ambitions, and also left him in no doubt about the fatal consequences of war.

The Boer War

A decade after the above remarks, Belloc faced a real war – The Boer War (now usually referred to as the 'South African War'). He did not like this

2   *Ibid,* p. 70
3   *Ibid,* p. 72
4   *Ibid,* p. 71

war and he did not support it; he believed Britain was in the wrong, and the Dutch republics in the right. In some ways his position was an unexpected one – the Boers being Calvinistic Protestants, were hardly his natural theological allies – but his sense of the war being more about control of gold and diamond mines than liberty and justice, as the British government claimed, riled and infuriated the thirty-year old Belloc.

Many of the men who had become his friends at Balliol were serving in the war. He longed to be with them as much as he longed for the war to end. These conflicted loyalties were expressed very starkly in two verses from his poem 'To the Balliol Men Still in Africa':

> I have said it before, and I will say it again,
> There was treason done, and a false word spoken,
> And England under the dregs of men,
> And bribes about, and a treaty broken:
> But angry, lonely, hating it still,
> I wished to be there in spite of the wrong.
> My heart was heavy for Cumnor Hill
> And the hammer of galloping all day long.
>
> Galloping outward into the weather,
> Hands a-ready and battle in all:
> Words together and wine together
> And song together in Balliol Hall.
> Rare and single! Noble and few! ...
> Oh! they have wasted you over the sea!
> The only brothers ever I knew,
> The men that laughed and quarrelled with me.[5]

First World War

When it came to the First World War, Belloc had no qualms; he had predicted the inevitability of war and indeed its necessity, as the united Germany was a nation dominated by Prussia with its martial mentality and its disdain for the cultural traditions of Europe:

5   Wilson, A.N., *Hilaire Belloc, Complete Verse* (Pimlico 1991), pp. 43 – 44

It is already half-mad. Before long we shall see it run amuck. And if we do not kill it, it will kill us. Prussia can no longer think widely, she cannot paint, she cannot write. And most of what Germany had patiently learnt from the civilised west and south through centuries of industrious pupillage, Prussia has tarnished or got rid of in no longer interval of time.[6]

The atrocities committed by the Germans, in the first weeks of the conflict in Belgium, galvanised public opinion in favour of the war. In our own times there is a general presumption that the Second World War was necessary in order to defeat the evil of Nazism, but that the First World War was an 'imperialist war' brought about by ruling elites vying for geopolitical dominance. This is not how it was seen at the time. Many on the left of British politics supported the war effort, including the syndicalist trade union leader, Ben Tillett, the same Ben Tillett who had inspired the young Belloc during the Great Dock Strike 25 years earlier: "Despite our former pacifist attitude," Tillett wrote, "the forces of labour in England have supported the government throughout the war. We realised that this is a fight for world freedom against a carefully engineered plan to establish world autocracy."[7]

Belloc was not impressed with the 'moderate socialists' who maintained their pacifist position: "Pale Ebenezer thought it wrong to fight, But Roaring Bill (who killed him) thought it right."[8] In a struggle against megalomania, the only options were war until victory or ignominious capitulation. Yet, despite this very pro-war position, Belloc was wholly opposed to conscription when it was introduced in 1916, believing it was both un-English and wrong.[9]

Belloc was probably most widely read during the First World War. His articles in *Land and Water*, a newspaper launched with the express

6   Speaight, *Ibid*, p. 352
7   The author has this quote among his hand-written notes from his college days, with no reference. He includes it here in the sure belief that the quote is accurate. Tillett's support for the war effort is confirmed in his entry on the socialist website, www. spartacus-educational.com
8   Wilson, *Complete Verse, ibid*, p. 118
9   Speaight, *ibid*, p. 366

intention of boosting the war effort, were read by hundreds of thousands, if not millions of people every week. He knew he was writing propaganda, he was also being paid very well for it (he would never earn as much again), and this must have troubled him, but not as much as losing the war troubled him. The confidence he displayed in his articles, that victory was close at hand, began to irk some of his readership as the casualties mounted and the months of war turned into years. The *Daily Mail* lambasted "Belloc's Fables,"[10] while an anonymous book was published, entitled, 'What I Know About the War,' by 'Blare Hilloc.' The pages of the book were entirely blank.[11]

In the years immediately preceding the war, Belloc had found himself surrounded by a small but close-knit group of supporters, who had rallied to his cause during the Marconi scandal. These men were, typically, ten to fifteen years younger than Belloc, which meant that they, unlike him, were of fighting age when war broke out in 1914. Belloc was in his mid-forties, they were in their twenties and thirties. As they began to become casualties of war, so the loss bore down heavily on Belloc. Someone meeting him for the first time, described meeting "old Mr Belloc,"[12] yet he was only 45! The death of Elodie had been an awful blow, but now the blows kept coming.

In March 1916, Basil Blackwood, home from the front, visited Belloc at King's Land, they reflected on those of their friends who had died. Belloc stared into the fire and murmured lines from Virgil, "vitaque cum gemitu fugit indignata sub umbras (and life fled with a groan, indignant, to the shadows)"[13] By the end of the following year, Blackwood himself would be dead, as would be Raymond Asquith, Edward Horner, and Auberon Herbert. Belloc was in France when he learned that Lucas had been lost in action, he wrote to G.K. Chesterton back in England:

> Pray for Bron Herbert continually and he will help you from heaven. I do not know how these things are … but in human words he was the most chivalrous, the bravest and the best, and he will help us all out of heaven.

10 *Ibid*, p. 349
11 Pearce, Jospeh, *Old Thunder, A Life of Hilaire Belloc* (Harper Collins 2002), p. 170
12 Wilson, A.N. *Hilaire Belloc* (Hamish Hamilton 1984), p. 221
13 Speaight, *ibid*, p. 369

God has received him with the fighting men of the Pyrenees whom he loved.[14]

To Juliet Duff, he wrote: "He was the noblest and the best and therefore they took him from this vile world, and our lives our changed."[15]

Cecil Chesterton was the last of this inner group to die. At the end of 1917, he was discharged from active service with a septic hand. When the Germans launched their great offensive in March 1918, he again volunteered and was accepted. Towards the end of the war he caught trench fever and was removed to a military hospital, where he died. A requiem service was held for him in England, where Father Vincent McNabb preached what Belloc judged to be the most outstanding eulogy he ever heard. Worse still, Belloc's son Louis was missing in action. His plane had gone down behind enemy lines, all the family hoped and prayed he had been taken prisoner. It was in a state of grief and anxiety that Belloc wrote these words in memory of Cecil Chesterton:

> His courage was heroic, native, positive, and equal: always at the highest potentiality of courage. He never in his life checked an action or a word from a consideration of personal caution, and that is more than can be said of any other man of his time.[16]

Having listed many other qualities, Belloc admitted, "the qualities I have described are less than the things which I have not said of such a friend and of such a companion in arms: tam cari capitis (our grief for a man so beloved)."[17]

Once the Armistice came into effect on 11th November 1918, all the Belloc family had renewed hope that news would reach them that Louis was safe and would soon return with other released prisoners of war. When no such news reached them by Christmas, it became increasingly clear that all hope was lost. In the New Year, Belloc went to France, hoping

14 *Ibid*, pp. 369 – 370
15 *Ibid*
16 *Ibid*, pp. 370 – 371
17 *Ibid*

to find news, but there was none. Slowly, Louis's brothers and sisters had to adjust to the cold truth that they would not see their brother again.

While in France, Belloc travelled to Metz, which had been under German rule since 1871, and saw how quickly all remnants of the German presence were being removed. A statue of Frederick the Great on horseback had been shorn of its rider, so that only the horse remained, "giving the impression that a grateful people [had] put up a statue to a horse,"[18] Belloc wryly noted. Even in the midst of grief, his humour did not desert him.

He also travelled to the Palatinate, whose population were German, but now found themselves under French occupation. Given the trauma of the last four years and all the pain of loss, and the most painful of all being so recent, Belloc displayed a remarkable lack of hatred towards the German population he encountered:

> The German people of the Palatinate and the Rhine have but one preoccupation, which is that the war is over. God never made them for battle. They do not hate nor do they love very much with their dull eyes: but they desire quiet and the French please them. They are all smiles and good will. They want their survivors, the prisoners, back again – especially the mothers. They vaguely regret the thefts and murders and worse that their armies foolishly incurred....But it took place far from them, and the same lack of vision makes them sentimental today. They are not one ounce Prussian. On the contrary they are hugely relieved of the Prussian strait-jacket. They are like a people who, at last, have been allowed to go to bed.[19]

How wonderful and vivid is that last phrase, full of human understanding and empathy. Belloc was only just coming to terms with the loss of his son, yet he does not clamour for vengeance, but wishes these Germans the peace of sleep. Surely this is Belloc at his most noble and most Christian?

More extraordinary, he was even able to feel compassion towards General Von Moltke, who suffered defeat at the Battle of Marne. Belloc spoke to those who had seen the famous military man in the heart of the old town at the moment he realised all was lost:

18 Speaight, Robert (Ed), *Letters From Hilaire Belloc* (Hollis & Carter), p. 90, letter to Juliet Duff
19 *Ibid*, p. 91, letter to Katherine Asquith

A group of boys playing in the square ceased from play to gaze at the old boy, timidly approaching the railings, and stared at the poor broken figure. They could know nothing of the tradition of the Prussian army, nor of how strange a sight they saw, but they felt its enormity. He, for his part, had forgotten what was around him – the place, the children; he stared at the ground, remembering as in a vivid dream his urgent appeal to his emperor, his agony at defeat, his intelligence too great for his heart, and the knell still ring there: 'the campaign has failed … the campaign has failed.'[20]

This anecdote reminds us that Belloc, for all his strong opinions and occasional rages, was not deaf to the cry of the human soul in torment, even when that soul belonged to an enemy. Von Moltke died shortly after his defeat.

Nor did Belloc forget the dead. For several years after the war, he arranged for a Mass to be held for all his friends who had died. He travelled again to France and entered into often arduous negotiations with church and cathedral authorities, to have plaques erected to the memory of these dear lost friends, at sites closest to where they had fallen, including one to his own son in Cambrai Cathedral. He regretted he had not spent more time with Louis, and he remembered the boat they had made together and sailed in before the war.

On this second visit, he went to his old family home in France and found it almost derelict. We can imagine how the dilapidated property would have reflected his deep sense of personal loss and sorrow:

It was a strange experience to find it still standing and only deserted – though suffering from a life-time of emptiness. It is thirty years since I last lived and slept there and 20 perhaps since it was regularly inhabited: it was astonishingly full of reminiscence and childhood. I used to go over as a child, every summer, from England to see my grandmother who lived there. Then gradually it fell into less and less use and was abandoned, but never sold. But perhaps it can hardly be lived in again.[21]

20 Speaight, *Life of Hilaire Belloc, ibid*, p. 473
21 Speaight, Letters, pp. 95 – 96, to Katherine Asquith

Belloc wrote this letter to Katherine Asquith, widow of Raymond, who had been killed in the war. Much of Belloc's correspondence for the remainder of his life was with the widows of friends he had lost. He was always there to be of assistance and help to these women and would write at great length on matters of loss and bereavement. Arguably his most deep and considered reflections on life, death and spiritual belief, were with Katherine Asquith[22] – a woman praised for her beauty and intelligence. The widowed Belloc never sought to be anything other than a loyal and attentive friend to her, as with the other women with whom he was in regular correspondence; this reveals to us a man of the utmost personal integrity, who remained ever constant and loyal to the memory of his own departed wife.

The Second World War

With Belloc, it is so easy to step with him from the sublime to the ridiculous. When we come to consider his position on the Second World War, we have to start with his attitude towards Hitler and the Nazis. As we have seen in the chapter on politics, Belloc consistently opposed the Nazis and their racial policies. As Robert Speaight has suggested, Belloc never really understood that the Nazis were far more malignant than just an updated version of old-style Prussian militarism, although perhaps modern historians and commentators underplay the connection? But having just seen Belloc at his elegiac best in his response to the Great War, we find him in 1932, being more than just a bit flippant, insulting and inaccurate in describing the electoral advances of the Nazis in Germany:

> The truth is that the party for immediate action, of which the wretched Hitler is a figure head and the clever Yid Rosenberg the manager, has not only a notable success but a big promise for the future.[23]

It is unlikely that any historian will be found today who would consider

22 *Ibid.*, in particular see his letter to her dated 16th July 1921, pp. 111 – 114
23 *Ibid*, p. 227, letter to Duff Cooper

Hitler a 'figure head' of the Nazi Party, or that Alfred Rosenberg was its 'clever manager.' Neither was Rosenberg, as Belloc seems to have assumed, a Jew, but rather a Baltic German. Rosenberg did run the Nazis' foreign affairs department and was considered to be of sufficient power and influence within the Nazi state to be tried and executed for war crimes and crimes against humanity at the Nuremberg trials in 1946.

Belloc has the habit of reacting to grave situations with levity; it appears to be one of his coping mechanisms (as we shall see in the next chapter). We should also appreciate that he was writing to a friend, not writing an article for publication. The cursory use of offensive racial expressions (although less offensive then than today), do little for his reputation; but this is Belloc, warts and all.

Belloc was certainly correct in assessing that "the party for immediate action" had a "promise for the future" – within a year the Nazis would be in power and within two, Hitler would have gained full dictatorial powers over his party, his country, and the military – some figurehead!

We have seen how Belloc denounced the Nazi 'monstrosity' and condemned Mussolini for passing Nazi-like racial laws in 1938. He also called for a military alliance between Britain and France against Germany, something he believed the pro-German elements within the British establishment were resisting. He believed much of the media and the academic establishment remained wedded to an Anglo-German alliance that even the rise to power of the Nazis could not dispel. Writing to a friend at the beginning of the war, when there was a real chance of invasion, Belloc returned to these themes:

> I trust that if the Germans come into your part of the country, you will shoot them without hesitation, in spite of the natural affinity between them and ourselves. The dons of my time always used to talk of our 'German Cousins.' The dons must be feeling very cold and lonely now, because there has passed a sudden wave of unpopularity over the Germans, and I find it difficult indeed to build up a new public feeling in their favour. But the position is heartbreaking for the *Daily News*, the *British Weekly* and many another Christian soul.[24]

24 *Ibid*, p. 300, letter to W.N. Roughhead

The fall of France in May 1940, followed by the collaboration of the Vichy government with the Nazis, was an unimaginable calamity for Belloc. J.B. Morton observed the impact it had on him:

> We talk of a 'stunning blow.' The adjective is the only one to use to describe the effect on Belloc of the defeat and collapse of France after so short a campaign. He was too bewildered and dazed to talk about it much. It was difficult to accept the fact that it had really happened.[25]

That autumn, the Battle of Britain raged, but Belloc was unbowed. He would not leave his home, despite its close proximity to the likely invasion location on the Sussex coast, nor would he desist from his regular visits to London. After one absence, he was shocked by the damage that the bombing had done to the city:

> I was appalled at the sight of London after ten days absence. What impressed me most was the burning down of St. James's church. I came on the firemen from the west of Piccadilly and saw them pumping water into the smouldering wreck. It is a monument for which I have always had respect and attachment. I have been to it so often for memorial services and what not and I loved its air of tradition.[26]

Two weeks later he was in Oxford, and noticed the mood of anxiousness and the suggestion of society beginning to fray at the edges:

> There has been a murder or two in Oxford and the food is worse than ever and the streets impassable through the enormous crush....There are also 2 or 3 regiments (the soldiers from which snatch handbags and knock-down old ladies in the blackout). The regular Oxfordians, scouts and shop employees and particularly barber's men, have gone all Bolshie. They resent wealth – to which hitherto they have crawled in the most abject manner – and they are therefore a nuisance, particularly the cab-men.[27]

These were not the words of a man looking to the future with confidence.

25 Morton, J.B., *A Memoir of Hilaire Belloc* (Hollis & Carter 1955), p. 159
26 *Ibid*, Speaight, Letters, p. 296, letter to Major-General Guy Dawnay
27 *Ibid*, p. 297, letter to Hon. Mrs Herbert

However civil society did not break down, nor did the threatened invasion materialise, although the possibility of it remained for at least another year. Then, in April 1941, came yet another blow; once again terrible grief arrived at Belloc's doorstep – news that his son, Peter, had been killed, training with the Marines in Scotland. For a man of seventy, having suffered so much loss in his lifetime, could he recover from this?

Belloc's daughter, Eleanor, assisted her father to prepare for the funeral. As she helped him on with his coat, he looked at her with a troubled frown, "Is it Louis or Peter?"[28] he asked. He was unsure which son he was burying. It was at this moment that Eleanor first realised that her father's formidable powers of recovery were deserting him. At the funeral, Belloc stood apart from the other mourners, alone with his thoughts.

For a time it seemed he might recover some of his old sparkle, that he would will himself to go on. He continued to write letters, including to his late son's friends serving in the Forces. He was relieved that the Pétain government in Vichy had not joined Germany in a military alliance against Britain, but was very disappointed that Marshall Pétain, a man he admired, should have made any sort of deal at all with the Germans. He wished he could find out what was really happening in France. He feared that the war was 'likely to end in some sort of compromise' with Hitler, 'But,' he continued, 'I'd rather die than talk or write publicly of compromise.'[29] He continued to write for those newspapers that would still take his articles.

He was able to be amused at the discomfort of his old bête noire, the wealthy families of England:

> The Rich, having discovered that the authorities will pay them anything for their houses, fell upon the Treasury like a pack of hounds and tore it to pieces. But note that there is a drawback to this gold mine: the army having taken over the rural places of the Rich, hammers nails into the walls, pulls down the rare and rich hangings, spits all over the floor and behaves, in general, like the brutal and licentious soldiery of which we read in our school-books.[30]

28 Wilson, *ibid*, p. 367
29 Speaight, Letters, *Ibid*, pp. 304 – 305
30 *Ibid*, p. 299, letter to R.N.Roughhead

Towards the end of 1941, he wrote to one of Peter's friends in the army. His style was still that mixture of outrageous exaggeration and human understanding:

> Write and tell me when you first come across a German officer prisoner and whether you find him intelligent or not. I never found one yet who was not a conceited and stuffed fool. But that perhaps is because all those I have seen have been German soldiers. The German left to himself is kindly and intelligent, though marvellously limited in the matter of information.[31]

> "England you will be glad to hear," he concluded, "goes plodding along from day to day and refuses to be disturbed. In this England is very wise".[32]

These are the last published words Belloc ever wrote. He suffered a stroke on 30th January 1942 and never wrote an article or letter again.

31 *Ibid*, p. 305
32 *Ibid*

The Winter of Life

REFLECTIONS ON YOUTH, OLD AGE AND DEATH

'You are old, Father William,' the young man said,
'And your hair has become very white;
And yet you incessantly stand on your head—
Do you think, at your age, it is right?'
LEWIS CARROLL

Even the poems Belloc wrote as a boy demonstrate a melancholic disposition, one that was aware, even at that early age, of the lurking spectre of mortality that shadows us all. He did not try and hide from this spectre nor pretend that ageing was a process that was anything more than the dissipation of youth; for which reason he always looked on the days of his young adulthood with joy and recommended to the rising generation that they should always seize the opportunities that life presented to them:

> When one is quite young then is the time to learn the world. One never learns it later. I have always been glad that I left school at 17, learnt to plow (*sic*), reap and sow, shot a lot, went off to America from east to west, walked all over California and Colorado, went into the French Artillery and got into Balliol and all before I was 22. Since then I have done nothing and those are the only years in which one lives; for one has no duties and no accursed conscience.[1]

Excepting the outrageous Bellocian hyperbole of having "done nothing" since he was 22, we can all remember the vibrancy of youth and the days when anything seemed possible. Although Belloc was not a sentimentalist;

---

1   Speaight, Robert, The *Life of Hilaire Belloc* (Hollis & Carter 1958), p. 33

from the standpoint of old age, he wondered at the liberty he enjoyed in those far off days, enjoying good company and revelling in the exuberance of it all:

> We laughed together a great deal; our conversation was extremely free; we ragged each other; and we sang at the top of our voices. We feasted and smoked together, we went out for walks and excursions, and nothing could have been happier or more high-spirited ....[2]

It was the memory of such times that he recalled in the opening verses of his poem, 'The Fire':

> We rode together all in pride,
> They laughing in their riding gowns
> We young men at their side,
> We charged at will across the downs.
>
> We were companions. We were young.
> We were immortal – so we said...
> For that which in the heart was sung
> Could have no commerce with the Dead.[3]

The poem concludes with old Belloc reflecting and remembering by his wintery fireside:

> Were they not here, the girls and boys?
> I hear them. They are at my call.
> The stairs are full of ghostly noise,
> But there is no one in the hall.
>
> The firelight sinks: a reddening shade:
> I watch alone beside the fire:
> The fire of my good oak is made:
> Where is the flower of my desire?

The 'flower' of his 'desire' may include much of what he had lost: his wife,

2   *Ibid*, p. 81
3   Wilson, A.N. (Ed), *Hilaire Belloc, Complete Verse*, pp. 78 – 79

his sons, his friends, or indeed his hope and desire for a world so different from the one he found himself living in during the 1930s. Belloc conjures up the dreaminess of reminiscence in his poem recalling a sultry night in Algeria:

In Barbary when I was young
A woman singing through the night,
The scented lemon trees among
In Barbary when I was young.

The song that in the night was sung,
By Lailah the Rahabite.
In Barbary when I was young,
A woman singing through the night.[4]

How Men Die

It was Belloc's ability to recall his youthful naivety without rancour that helped him battle on in later life. He certainly did not "go quietly into that good night," as J.B. Morton recalled:

He knew, as any intelligent man knows, that what we are all seeking is not to be found in the brief years on earth. That habit of complaining, and of saying life was a disgusting thing, was like the vigorous protests of a sailor in a storm or a soldier under shell-fire. It helped him to go on with what he had to do. At the end of his life, when he had leisure to think over his disappointments, when he was suffering physically and mentally, he bore his burden with patience and resignation.[5]

We saw in earlier chapters how land and the sea had a profound effect on Belloc. The metaphor of landscape and seascape is a recurring devise in his writings. He used it to good effect while visiting East Anglia, to summon up different types of men and their different ways of dying, for

4   *Ibid*, p. 79
5   Morton, J.B., *A Memoir of Hilaire Belloc* (Hollis & Carter 1955), pp. 10 – 11

death was never far from Belloc's mind, and the way men lived, Belloc believed, had a great bearing on the way men died:

> The coasts of western England are like the death of a western man in battle – violent and heroic. The land dares all, and plunges into a noisy sea. The coast of eastern England is like the death of one of these eastern merchants here – lethargic, ill-contended, drugged with ease. The dry land slips, and wallows into a quiet, very shallow water, confused with yellow thickness and brackish with the weight of inland water behind.[6]

Belloc at 60

On reaching 60, Belloc was still plunging into the noisy seas of controversy and certainly showed no sign of becoming 'drugged with ease.' His friends held a great party for him. It was an uproarious affair, with much drinking, singing and good humour. Belloc joked that by 60, a man no longer cared what people thought about his work, although he had heard that men began to care very much again for their reputation on reaching 70, in which case, he declared, he hoped he would die at 69! Despite his high spirits and the continued presence of good and loving friends, Morton could see that the years were taking their toll:

> At this time Belloc looked much older than his sixty years. Overwork, lack of sleep, and no settled way of living were telling on him more and more. Yet in the years that followed he worked even harder than before, pouring out novels and essays and articles and books of all kinds. But if we noticed any increased fatigue, it was only because of what he had been before. His vitality was still that of a man of forty, and, for all his complaints, was apparently inexhaustible.[7]

He did complain incessantly to his friends about the realities of ageing, but he always did it with humour and self-deprecation. In 1932 he was

---

6 Belloc, Hilaire, *The Hills and the Sea* (Methuen & Co. 1927, originally published in 1906), p. 112
7 *Ibid*, p. 79

lamenting the condition of his eyesight: "I wish you had sent me some new eyes for Christmas. When you do send them let them be of a liquid brown, for I am tired of having pale green eyes. I got them when I was quite young and did not know how unfashionable they are."[8]

In July 1940, with the commencement of the Battle of Britain only weeks away, Belloc was desperately trying to get one of the national newspapers to take his articles, but he was not the figure he had been when war broke out in 1914, and he had spent much of the intervening years attacking the character and the motives of the men who owned these newspapers. He wrote to Mary Herbert, whose father-in-law was the Earl of Carnarvon, wondering if she could use her influence to get him some paid employment: "In the *Land and Water* days of the Great War I controlled the whole paper; today I have to consider others who control. This is entirely due to poverty. I hope you will do what you can to make one of the remaining millionaires endow me, for I am getting old, as the port said. But the wine was boasting, whereas I am complaining."[9]

Morton also became aware of how Belloc, in company, would mask his sadness with displays of bravado; partly so as not to depress his friends, and partly so as not to depress himself:

> It was some time before I realized that Belloc was an unhappy and a disappointed man. His habit of expressing discontents in such an amusing way made it difficult to disentangle the genuine bitterness from the jests. Yet there was no mystery in this seeming contradiction in his character. He was a man of robust health and strong will who, when trapped into exposing his deeper feelings, regained his balance, as it were, before you had noticed what had happened. He enjoyed the good things of life in the heartiest manner, and was far too sane to allow personal grievances or misfortunes to interfere with good company. I remember a man saying to him: 'So your old friend Philip Kershaw is dead.' He said, 'Yes.' And was silent for a moment. Then he burst into song, and everyone joined in. That was, I think, the first time that I was not deceived.[10]

8   Speaight, *Ibid*, p. 515
9   Speaight, Robert (Ed), *Letters from Hilaire Belloc* (Hollis & Carter), p. 291
10   Morton *ibid*, p. 118

Young Friends in Old Age

It suited Belloc well to have young friends. In his days at the *New Witness*, many of his friends were ten or more years younger than him; in the 1930s, men such as Morton and Dermod MacCarthy, were 30 or 40 years younger. He still had friends from his youth, such as Maurice Baring, but it was his young friends that gave him hope and replenished his energy levels, when his latest battle with politicians, college dons, or newspaper proprietors had depleted them. It is from these younger friends that we have such wonderful accounts of Belloc, a man whom they all revered and respected, and whose views and beliefs shaped their own for the rest of their lives.

Morton, in particular, has recorded for us Belloc's ability to produce a verse or song on the spur of the moment, or sing an old song that amused him. "There was," Morton tells us, "a certain unprintable eighteenth century ditty, called *The Parson and the Crayfish*, which he was liable to sing in all but the politest company."[11] On one occasion, rather than discuss the finer details of the Tudor court of Henry VIII any longer, he turned to verse:

> Anne Boleyn had no breeches to wear,
> So the king got a sheepskin and cut her a pair;
> Skin side out and woolly side in –
> It was warm in the summer for Anne Boleyn.[12]

Belloc also loved to sing Music Hall songs, one of his favourites being *If It Wasn't for the 'Ouses in Between* by Gus Elen. Morton wasn't sure if the following Belloc favourite was from the Music Hall or Belloc's own composition:

> O father, dear father, come home to us now,
> For we want your breeches to pawn,
> The cat has had kittens and run up the flue,
> And the row in the house has begun.

---

11   *Ibid*, p. 9, almost certainly a variant of the very explicit 'Crabfish Song.'
12   *Ibid*, p. 43

Come ho-o-ome! Come ho-o-home!
Mother is waiting to welcome you in
Behind the door with a rolling-pin –
O father, dear father, come home![13]

A Google-search revealed that this was originally a serious and sentimental mid-nineteenth century temperance song, warning of the evils of drink on family life. We know what Belloc thought of the 'Lord Rumbo' and 'Pale Ebernezers' who wagged their fingers at the bad behaviour of the working classes, so it's not surprising to find him mocking their moral crusading. Morton understood this aspect of Belloc very well:

> His sense of humour was unfailing. It was not merely the ability to make a joke or to appreciate somebody else's joke. It was a sane and healthy way of looking at life, so that he never attached undue importance to what is relatively unimportant. His sense of humour was not dependent on a mood. It was not a matter of being in good spirits. It was there and active, all the time, playing like a fountain. His enjoyment of the comedy of human existence prevented him from becoming too embittered, and kept him essentially simple. As words are used today, he would be called sophisticated, and a compliment would be intended. He knew the world's usage and the motives of men. But in the older and true meaning of the word, he was not sophisticated: that is, his knowledge and wide experience had not warped or adulterated his nature.[14]

Even Belloc's humour could be layered with the existential doubt that was never dispelled from his mind. He might be performing on the stage of Catholic Truth, but lurking in the wings, his active mind was always questioning:

Am I a man or am I a mouse?
Am I a hedger or a dodger?
I should bloody well like to know

13 *Ibid*
14 *Ibid*, p. 10

> Who's running this damned show –
> Is it me or the top floor lodger?[15]

Meryvn Herbert was with Belloc when he was arrested by Spanish border police, for allegedly calling one of the officers an idiot. After eight hours in the cells and an urgent telegram to the British ambassador in Madrid, Belloc was released.[16] In a letter to a friend about the incident, he revealed that this was the fifth time he had been arrested and placed "in the hands of the police,"[17] the previous occasions being in Oxford, Folkestone, Calestaro in Italy, and Luko in the Ukraine. It is to be doubted if any of Belloc's literary contemporaries – Wells, Shaw, or Eliot – could have claimed the same. Belloc was certainly not 'sophisticated' when it came to dealing with policemen or other state functionaries.

The insomnia that had blighted Belloc's adult life did not diminish in his 60s, although he learned to accept the affliction: "I used to get myself into a frenzy of effort to seize on sleep, but now I just lie awake and bear it and I find it wearies me less."[18] However, he did start to experience periods of memory loss, which would probably be identified today as TIAs, or mini strokes:

> It was a dreadful thing that happened. I completely lost my memory. I had a very bad night, and when I got up this morning, I was rather dazed and I remained so during the morning. I tried to do some work in the library of the Reform Club, and I went on till half-past one, and then went off to lunch with my mind quite empty. This sort of thing has happened to me once or twice in the last two or three years. It does not seem to get more frequent, but it is really alarming when it does happen, and distresses me a great deal. It comes of having done more work than I ought to have done at my age.[19]

15 Morton, *ibid*, p. 28
16 Speaight, *Life of Hilaire Belloc, ibid*, p. 463
17 Speaight, Letters, *ibid*, pp. 154 – 155, letter to Katherine Asquith
18 Speaight, *Life of Hilaire Belloc, ibid*, p. 515
19 Morton *ibid*, pp. 132 – 133

As well as periodic memory loss, Belloc also started to have attacks of vertigo: "I was alarmed and depressed by these two fits of vertigo. It made me feel that anything might happen and that one was not safe crossing the streets."[20] He lamented that "one is much older in body than the mind will accept," and that "one does not pick up again at once and as a matter of course."[21] None of this stopped him continuing to sail with his young friends, although Dermod MacCarthy remembered the concern that they all had for him at sea:

> His tiredness and his giddiness recurred, however, and between ourselves we began to say 'ought he to go on?' Perhaps our worries were exaggerated. He knew himself better than we did. But one day when I was alone with him, I had an awful moment when I thought Mr Belloc was dying. We had gone ashore without him and he stayed on board to read or sleep. I came back before the others and stepped aboard quietly from the quayside. I sat on the hatch cover for a while inspecting the decks and rigging with my eye. Suddenly I heard a sound like heavy breathing coming from the cabin: it took me a few moments to decide if the sound was human or not. They were long husky hollow sounds, rather like a broken-winded horse but slower. What on earth was happening? In two leaps I was down the hatchway. There was Mr Belloc blowing up his great rubber mattress with his own breath.
>
> 'My dear, I'm so glad you've arrived. That little contraption' – pointing to the small concertina-like bellows that was supposed to do the job – 'is no use to man or beast – I'm trying to blow the thing up with my own lungs, which are ten times better than it, even at my age – the valve keeps leaking.'
>
> 'Sir, I thought you were dying!' I said, which produced a burst of laughter. 'well – you might have been right, my dear, you might have been right!'[22]

20 Speaight, Letters, *ibid*, p. 242, letter to Mrs Balfour
21 *Ibid.*
22 MacCarthy, Dermod, *Sailing with Mr Belloc* (Grafton Books, 1986, originally published in 1925), p. 132

Mortality and Consolation

Belloc himself, in private and thoughtful mood, continually pondered on life and its ending. Although of deep faith himself, he never condemned another man for his belief or disbelief, although the arrogance of others who did condemn or dismiss, greatly troubled him. We were all on the same path and we should all have the good sense to listen to the wisdom of others:

> There is no man who has closely inquired upon this, and there is none who has troubled himself and admitted a reasonable anxiety upon it, who has not well retained the nature of despair. Those who approach their fellow-beings with assertion and violence in such a matter, affirming their discovery, their conviction, or their acquired certitude, do an ill service to their kind. It is not thus that the last things should be approached, nor the most tremendous problem which man is doomed to envisage, be propounded and solved. Ah! The long business of this world! The way in which your deepest love goes up in nothingness and breaks away, and the way in which the strongest and the most continuous element of your life is dissipated, and fails you in some moment; if I do not understand these things in a man, nor comprehend how the turn of the years can obscure or obliterate a man's consciousness of what is and should be, then I act in brute ignorance, or, what is much worse, in lack of charity.[23]

One lesson he believed he had learned, was that there were two ways to live a life to its fullest, and yet they were such different paths as to appear like polar opposites:

> Look you, good people all, in your little passage through the daylight, get to see as many hills and buildings and rivers, fields, books, men, horses, ships and precious stones as you can possibly manage to do. Or else stay in one village and marry in it and die there. For one of these two fates is the best fate for every man. Either to be what I have been, a wanderer with all the bitterness of it, or to stay at home and hear in one's garden the voice of God.[24]

23 Belloc, Hilaire, *On Something* (Methuen 1918), pp. 11 – 12
24 *Ibid*, p. 98

In the previous chapter we considered the time, advice and consideration Belloc gave to the young widows who had lost their husbands in the Great War; perhaps there was no letter he ever wrote more full of empathy, love and caring for the soul of another human being, than that which he wrote to Lady Laura Lovat on hearing the news of the death of her young son. This letter demonstrates all that was good and gracious in his character, rather than the harsh words and sarcasm that often marked his dealings with 'the world' at this time, in the 1930s. "I have been thinking of you continually all these long weeks," he writes, "desiring to know how you were, yet hesitating to write." Maurice Baring, their mutual friend, had convinced Belloc that he should write. He tells Lady Lovat that it is a letter "so long thought" and begins by telling her of the birth of his eldest son, Peter: "All my life since my first boy was born (the one who was killed at the end of the war) I have been vividly alive to what was meant by the ordeal of giving birth to a child," he explains, before seeking to face with her the terrible grief she is experiencing:

That is 35 years ago now, and ever since that major thing, that thing which women go through, has taken up my mind. Then later, I came to know as reality also death. Death is two-faced. It is the entry into Beatitude and the dereliction for a time of those who remain. But the bearing of children is also two-fold, for it is a mighty work of God, a direct claim upon Heaven, because of its anguish and a blessing here even in the fruition. God bless you. You must remember there are two kinds of suffering; the good and the bad; but the good creates glory and a claim on the justice of God. It is we who do not suffer who can make no such claim. God is in debt to you, and I believe He is one of those large spenders who pay lavishly – often late as is the way of spendthrifts – but lavishly. And having no limit to his wealth – unlike us who are so badgered by limits to wealth – He can pour it out. Masses of it will come your way unendingly. We who cannot say the same are filled with dull envy. If we shall have beatitude, we who do not suffer, and risk nothing, we shall have it à compte-gouttes [drop by small drop], as they used to say reproachfully of Brandy in the Army Canteens of my youth; but we ought to be grateful for the luck, if we can get it at all – even little drops of it. God bless you again.[25]

25 Speaight, Letters, *ibid*, p. 231

With gentle humour and sincere conviction, he holds out his hands to Lady Lovat, promising not to let go. It was because of true friendship such as this, that those who knew and loved Belloc forgave him his momentary furies and his exaggerated expressions of outrage, for they knew that, deep down, this was a Man of God, however flawed and imperfect. As he wrote in a letter to Katherine Asquith: "It is the only *really* important thing in the world, this understanding of Life and Death."[26]

Still Laughing at the World (and Himself)

On his last visit to America, in 1937, Belloc found that editors still wanted his articles, although they didn't want them the way he wrote them, as he explained in one of his letters, they wanted it "to be quite short," for which they were prepared to pay "a large sum of money," something the increasingly cash-poor Belloc appreciated:

> I sent [the editor] the article which was written after my usual style and was about Communism. He then sent me word by a friend and not by writing that he would like to change the article so as to make it more easily understood because I had made it too high brow. I told him to change anything he liked. He then changed it into words of one syllable and sentences not more than ten words long. It was like 'Reading Without Tears.' 'The fat cat is on the mat. There is a rat on the mat. The rat is in the cat. The fat cat is still on the mat.' In this way he made it comprehensible to his public ....[27]

Although he did not know it, Belloc was witnessing the birth of what we would call today 'tabloid journalism.' He did notice that America was becoming less and less like Europe: "the United States are so utterly different from us that we have difficulty in following their contemporary history," he noted, adding, "I am fond of them and get on with them – but it is like being on the moon."[28]

26   *Ibid*, p. 113
27   *Ibid*, p. 291, letter to Mary Herbert
28   Morton *ibid*, p. 153

As Belloc approached his 70th birthday, it was an anniversary shadowed by the clouds of war. There would be no gathering of friends as there had been for his sixtieth birthday. Many of his older friends were dead or incapacitated and his younger friends were fighting with the Armed Forces or engaged in other war work. The previous year, James Gunn had painted Belloc, which picture formed part of a private viewing for invited guests: "it made a great sensation," quipped Belloc, "for it is a most remarkable picture of the Gorilla Type."[29]

Ailments and maladies were mounting attacks on him from all fronts, and the 'golden years' were not what people hoped and expected:

> It is all due to Old Age, which is, I do assure you, the most horrible lingering (and incurable disease ever pupped or calved). It's funny that all the books lie so terribly about it. To read the books one would think that old age was a lovely interlude between the pleasures of this life and Beatitude. The book represents Old Age seated in a fine comfortable dignified chair, with venerable snowy locks and fine, wise, thoughtful eyes, a gentle but profound smile, and God-knows-what-all! But the reality is quite other. Old Age is a tangle of Disappointment, Despair, Doubt, Dereliction, Dropping, and Damnable Deficiency and everything else that begins with D.[30]

Belloc rather thought that modern medicine was prolonging life at the expense of good living:

> Of old when folk lay sick and sorely tried
> The doctors gave them physic, and they died.
> But here's a happier age: for now we know
> Both how to make men sick and keep them so.[31]

What he would have made of people today lingering for years in care homes, we hardly need to wonder; yet Belloc himself would linger in ill-health for nearly twelve years, from the stroke he suffered in January 1942 until his death in August 1953.

29 Speaight, Letters, *ibid*, p. 275, letter to Mary Herbert
30 Pearce, Joseph, *Old Thunder, A Life of Hilaire Belloc* (Harper Collins, 2002), p. 265
31 Wilson, *Verse*, *ibid*, p. 112

He probably had a sense of what was coming. To Juliet Duff, to whom he wrote many verses of dedication, he penned some final lines:

> One that was pledged, and goes to his replevining:
> One that now leaves with averted face
> A shadow passing through the doors at evening
> To his companion and his resting place.[32]

Juliet Duff may have been his muse and his romantic fantasy, but it was to Elodie – 'his companion' – to whom he was returning.

His Last Years

It is sad but necessary to recount the descriptions of Belloc in his dotage, for though we cannot but mourn the loss of such a vibrant and active mind, we can still learn from his example, of how to contend with decrepitude of mind and body and anticipate that eventuality.

Robert Speaight said that Belloc at this last stage of life "was like a great wind that had blown itself out into the calm of a summer evening."[33] J.B. Morton remembered sitting with him at King's Land, and although there were now longer silences between the two men, there was still the laughter and the songs as of past days.[34] He remembered Belloc singing:

> You with your teeth that hardly fit,
> And you with your idiot grin,
> Open wide those heavenly gates
> And let poor Hilary in,
> Poor old Hilary, dear old Hilary,
> Let poor Hilary in.[35]

Malcolm Muggeridge and Aubron Herbert visited him in December 1950:

32 *Ibid*, p. 107
33 Speaight, *Life of Hilaire Belloc*, *ibid*, p. 1
34 Morton *ibid*, p. 20
35 *Ibid*, p. 41

Belloc came shuffling in, walks with great difficulty because he has had a
stroke, inconceivably dirty ... mutters to himself and easily forgets what he
said, heavily bearded, fierce-looking and angry ... the fearful wilfulness of
the very old when they are not reconciled. The will still beating against the
bars, and the strokes becoming more frenzied and futile as they become
feebler....thought of King Lear. Belloc occasionally hummed snatches of
French songs, and then burst into what must have been a music hall song
when he was young – 'chase me girls, I've got a banana, oh what a banana!'
This song pleased him hugely .... When his daughter and grandson were
out of the room, he turned to Aubron and me and said: 'They're longing for
me to die!" and then laughed gleefully.[36]

Ironically, Muggeridge, many decades later, would end up in the same
condition as Belloc. Others who visited Belloc at this time remember an
old man who would still kneel and say his prayers in the chapel and take
communion, before which he would always light a candle. "The religious
silence would be broken only by the creaking of his bones when kneeling
or rising from prayer," one recalled.[37]

Evelyn Waugh and his wife visited in September 1952:

Sounds of shuffling. Enter old man, shaggy white beard .... Thinner than I
last saw him, with benevolent gleam. Like an old peasant or fisherman in a
French film. We went to greet him at a door. Smell like fox. He kissed Laura's
hand. I have known him quite well for nearly 20 years. It was slightly
disconcerting to be greeted with a deep bow and the words, 'It is a great
pleasure to make your acquaintance, Sir.' Shuffled to chair by the fire.
During the whole visit he was occupied with unsuccessful attempts to light
an empty pipe. He wore black broad cloth garnished with garbage,
enormous labourer's boots and open collar. I in rather smart and
conventional tweeds. He squinted at me for some time and said: 'we all wear
exactly the same clothes nowadays ....

36 Pearce, *ibid*, p. 281
37 *Ibid*, p. 282

He noticed my stick near the door and told the boys to put it away. Also a leaf that had blown in, which he expelled. He looked very hard at Laura and said, 'You are very like your mother, are you not?'

'She is taller.'

'English women are enormous. So are the men – giants. I am short.'

'Are you Sir, I am not able to judge.' He could not follow anything said to him but enjoyed pronouncing the great truths which presumably he ponders.[38]

When, in March 1953, when H.S. Mackintosh, an admirer of Belloc, came to visit Belloc in the company of Sir William Hayley, editor of *The Times*, they expected a meeting much like the ones described by Waugh and Muggeridge:

> The old man was, however, in great form, and before lunch started he was already reciting his own verse and singing his own songs. During lunch he discussed a variety of topics and, though his memory was failing and he became abstracted from time to time, his courtesy never faltered. Both Sir William and I are grateful for the memory of that last pilgrimage.[39]

Nearly thirty years earlier, Belloc had visited Thomas Hardy when that great novelist and poet was at the end of his life. Despite their very differing religious outlooks, Belloc treated the old man with the utmost respect, and the two found common interest in recounting memories of a storm that wrecked ships off the Dorset coast many years before.[40] The behaviour of the very old when mentally impaired is rather like that of small children, if we want to get the best out of them we need to treat them with love and consideration, not mockery.

Speaking to the Oxford Union in 1924, Belloc had said, in regards to posterity:

---

38 Wilson, *Hilaire Belloc, ibid*, pp. 384 – 385
39 Pearce, *ibid*, p. 263
40 Speaight, *Life of Hilaire Belloc, ibid*, pp. 490 – 491

I said to myself – if you want to be remembered after you are dead, you
must get a poet to write about you. But then I said to myself, why should
you want to be remembered after you are dead? And to that question I said
to myself, I can't imagine.[41]

Belloc never wrote or began an autobiography, nor did he keep any notes
suggesting he ever intended to write such a thing – in sharp contrast to
most his literary contemporaries. He has left us his verse, from among
which,we can find evidence to show that he cared little for posterity or the
vanities and snares so beguiling to mortal men.

Juliet Duff had distracted him and he was pleased of her company and
her attention, but he never deluded himself as to his enduring presence in
the memory of the young aristocrat:

> Towards the evening of her splendid day
> Those who are little children now shall say
> (Finding this verse), 'Who wrote it, Juliet?'
> And Juliet answer gently, 'I forget.'[42]

Without the hope of salvation in the next life, we are left only with the
unfair spoils of this one:

> Life is a long discovery, isn't it?
> You only get your wisdom bit by bit.
> If you have luck you find in early youth
> How dangerous it is to tell the Truth;
> And next you learn how dignity and peace
> Are the ripe fruits of patient avarice.
> You find that middle life goes racing past.
> You find despair: and, at the very last,
> You find as you are giving up the ghost
> That those who loved you best despised you most.[43]

---

41 *Ibid*, p. 470
42 Wilson, *Verse, ibid*, 'A Fragment,' p. 117
43 *Ibid*, 'Discovery,' p. 80

Last Word

I could have written here about the great controversies of our own times and what Belloc's attitude might have been towards them. Actually, I did write something, but on reflection, it struck me as a bit preachy, if not rather ranting. I am sure every reader can decide for themselves what Belloc might think of our modern world, after all, he had predicted many of the challenges we are now facing.

Instead I have decided to end with one of his poems and a joyful reminscence of Belloc at his most mischevious. The poem is one of his best known and most loved, 'Tarantella'. No one seems able to prove whether the 'Miranda' of the poem was a female companion of Belloc's, the Duke of Miranda, or a fictional woman he created to give focus and feeling to his poem. It hardly matters. What matters is that it is classic Belloc: it combines the joy of living, the exuberance of youthful good company with the concurrent awareness of the impermanence of all living things and the inevitable advance of death. It is not a duality that many of us care to acknowledge, but it is the inescapable truth of our existence.

> Do you remember an Inn,
> Miranda?
> Do you remember at Inn?
> And the tedding and the spreading
> Of the straw for a bedding,
> And the fleas that tease in the High Pyrenees,
> And the wine that tasted of the tar?
> And the cheers and the jeers of the young muleteers
> (Under the vine of the dark verandah)?
> Do you remember an Inn, Miranda,
> Do you remember an Inn?

And the cheers and the jeers of the young muleteers
Who hadn't got a penny,
And who weren't paying any,
And the hammer at the doors and the Din?
And the Hip! Hop! Hap!
Of the clap
Of the hands to the twirl and the swirl
Of the hand to the twirl and the swirl
Of the girl gone chancing,
Glancing,
Dancing,
Backing and advancing,
Snapping of a clapper to the spin
Out and in –
And the Ting, Tong, Tang of the Guitar!
Do you remember an Inn,
Miranda?
Do you remember an Inn!
Never more;
Miranda,
Never More.
Only the high peaks hoar:
And Aragon a torrent at the door.[1]
No sound
In the walls of the Halls where falls
The tread
Of the feet of the dead to the ground
No sound:
But the boom
Of the far Waterfall like Doom.

1   The reference to 'Aragon,' is to the river of that name, not the province. 'The
    Tarantella' is a traditional Pyrenean dance. Otis Kirby-Dunkley can be heard singing a
    rap version of Tarantella at https://belloc-broadwood.org.uk/
    tarantella-for-the-21st-century/

In seems a shame to leave Belloc with the 'Waterfall of Doom,' so let us remember him in joyful mood with his friends. Here Lord Stanley of Alderney remembers coming ashore with Belloc and his motley crew at Poole, and how Belloc led them straight ashore, determined that they should enjoy all that the town had to offer –

Moreover, nothing would satisfy Belloc but that a certain inn was "the best in Europe," and that consequently it would be a crime to pass it by. So, in due course, we found ourselves at the inn, which proved to be a rather down-at-heel commercial travellers way-call. The proprietor, seeing our disreputable appearance, made haste to tell us that his establishment was not for the likes of us, and that there was a hostelry more suited to our station and pockets a little further down the street. Belloc was at once in arms. He informed the inn-keeper in sonorous and rounded periods that I, his friend was "a Peer of the Realm and immensely rich." The good man, though somewhat troubled at the manner and the tone in which he was thus harangued by Belloc, thought he was being trifled with and briskly bade us be off. I, somewhat embarrassed by Belloc's importunate insistence, drew the owner aside and explained that, of course, as he could well see, I was not a Peer of the Realm, but that my friend was a Mr. Belloc, a distinguished man of letters, whose eccentricities were notorious. This the man believed for I think we accorded with his conception of what poor scribblers should look like, and he accordingly bade us welcome. Belloc was delighted when I explained how I had saved the day ....[2]

2   Introduction by Lord Stanley to *The Cruise of the Nona* (Constable & Co. Ltd 1955), pp xxiii - xxiv

Bibliography

Boyle, David, *Distributism and the politics of life* (The Real Press 2019)

Browne, Peter Francis, *Rambling the Road to Rome* (Sommersdale Publishers 2001)

Haynes, Reneé, *Hilaire Belloc* (Longmans, Green & Co 1953)

Copper, Bob, Across Sussex with *Belloc* (Alan Sutton Publishing 1994)

Flint, Nick, *Cautionary Pilgrim, Walking Backwards with Belloc* (Country Books/ Ashridge Press 2014)

Pearce, Joseph, *Old Thunder, A Life of Hilaire Belloc* (Harper Collins 2002)

Speaight, Robert, *The Life of Hilaire Belloc* (Hollis & Carter 1957)

Speaight, Robert Ed), *Letters from Hilaire Belloc* (Hollis & Carter 1958)

MacCarthy, Dermod, *Sailing with Mr Belloc* (Grafton Books 1986),

Morton, J.B., *Hilaire Belloc, A Memoir* (Hollis & Carter 1955)

Wilhelmsen, *Hilaire Belloc, No Alienated Man* (Sheed and Ward 1954)

West Sussex Library Service, *The Path to Rome, the life and works of Hilaire Belloc, in celebration of his life, on the occasion of the fiftieth anniversary of his death* (West Sussex County Council 2003)

Wilson, A.N., *Hilaire Belloc* (Hamish Hamilton 1984)

Wilson, A.N. (Ed), *Hilaire Belloc, Complete Verse* (Pimlico 1991)

Books and Pamphlets by Hilaire Belloc

The following list of Belloc's publications is taken from *The English First Editions of Hilaire Belloc* by Patrick Cahill. It is a fine piece of bibliographical scholarship, and should be consulted by anyone who wishes to have a full picture of Belloc's literary activity.

1896   VERSES AND SONNETS. Ward and Downey.

1896   THE BAD CHILD'S BOOK OF BEASTS. Oxford: Alden and Co., Bocardo Press; London: Simpkin, Marshall, Hamilton, Kent and Co.

1897   MORE BEASTS (FOR WORSE CHILDREN). Edward Arnold.

1898   THE MODERN TRAVELLER. Edward Arnold.

1899   DANTON. James Nisbet and Co.

1899   A MORAL ALPHABET. Edward Arnold.

1899   Extracts from the Diaries and Letters of HUBERT HOWARD with a Recollection by a Friend. (Edited by H.B.). Oxford: Horace Hart.

1900   LAMBKIN'S REMAINS. Oxford: The Proprietors of the J.C.R.

1900   PARIS. Edward Arnold.

1901   ROBESPIERRE. James Nisbet and Co.

1902   THE PATH TO ROME. George Allen.

1903   CALIBAN'S GUIDE TO LETTERS. Duckworth and Co.

1903   THE GREAT INQUIRY. Duckworth and Co.

1903   WHY EAT? A Broadside.

1903   THE ROMANCE OF TRISTAN AND ISEULT. Translated from the French of J. Bedier by H.B. George Allen.

1904   AVRIL. Duckworth and Co.

1904 EMMANUEL BURDEN. Methuen and Co.
1904 THE OLD ROAD. Archibald Constable
      and Co.
1906 ESTO PERPETUA. Duckworth and Co.
1906 AN OPEN LETTER ON THE DECAY OF
      FAITH. Bums and Oates.
1906 SUSSEX. Adam and Charles Black.
1906 HILLS AND THE SEA. Methuen and Co.
1907 THE HISTORIC THAMES.]. M. Dent
      and Co.
1907 CAUTIONARY TALES FOR CHILDREN.
      Eveleigh Nash.
1908 THE CATHOLIC CHURCH AND
      HISTORICAL TRUTH (Catholic Evidence
      Lectures, No. 3). Preston: W. Watson
      and Co.
1908 ON NOTHING. Methuen and Co.
1908 Mr. CLUTTERBUCK'S ELECTION.
      Eveleigh Nash.
1908 THE EYE-WITNESS. Eveleigh Nash.
1908 AN EXAMINATION OF SOCIALISM.
      Catholic Truth Society.
1909 THE PYRENEES. Methuen and Co.
1909 A CHANGE IN THE CABINET. Methuen
      and Co.
1909 MARIE ANTOINETTE. Methuen and Co.
1909 ON EVERYTIDNG. Methuen and Co.
1909 THE CHURCH AND SOCIALISM. Catholic
      Truth Society.
1910 THE FERRER CASE. Catholic Truth
      Society.
1910 ON ANYTHING. Constable and Co.
1910 PONGO AND THE BULL. Constable and
      Co.
1910 ON SOMETHING. Methuen and Co.
1910 VERSES. Duckworth and Co.
1911 THE PARTY SYSTEM, by Hilaire Belloc
      and Cecil Chesterton. Stephen Swift.
1911 THE FRENCH REVOLUTION. Williams
      and Norgate.
1911 THE GIRONDIN. Thomas Nelson and
      Sons.
1911 MORE PEERS. Stephen Swift.
1911 SOCIALISM AND THE SERVILE STATE.
      A Debate between Messrs. Hilaire
      Belloc and J. Ramsay MacDonald, M.P.
      The South West London Federation of
      the Independent Labour Party.
1911 FIRST AND LAST. Methuen and Co.
1912 THE BATTLE OF BLENHEIM. Stephen
      Swift and Co.

1912 MALPLAQUET. Stephen Swift and Co.
1912 WATERLOO. Stephen Swift and Co.
1912 THE FOUR MEN. Thomas Nelson
      and Sons.
1912 THE GREEN OVERCOAT. Bristol: J.
      W. Arrowsmith ; London: Simpkin,
      Marshall, Hamilton, Kent and Co.
1912 TURCOING. Stephen Swift and Co.
1912 WARFARE IN ENGLAND. Williams and
      Norgate.
1912 THIS AND THAT. Methuen and Co.
1912 THE SERVILE STATE. T. N. Foulis.
1912 THE RIVER OF LONDON. T. N. Foulis.
1912 CRÉCY. Stephen Swift and Co.
1913 THE STANE STREET. Constable and Co.
1913 POITIERS. Hugh Rees.
1914 ANTI-CATHOLIC HISTORY. Catholic
      Truth Society.
1914 THE BOOK OF THE BAYEUX TAPESTRY.
      Chatto and Windus.
1915 LAND & WATER MAP OF THE WAR,
      drawn under the direction of Hilaire
      Belloc. Land & Water.
1915 THE HISTORY OF ENGLAND (in eleven
      volumes). Vol. XI is by H. B. Sands
      and Co.; New York: The Catholic
      Publication Society of America.
1915 A GENERAL SKETCH OF THE EUROPEAN
      WAR: THE FIRST PHASE. Thomas Nelson
      and Sons.
1915 THE TWO MAPS OF EUROPE. C. Arthur
      Pearson.
1916 THE LAST DAYS OF THE FRENCH
      MONARCHY. Chapman and Hall.
1916 A GENERAL SKETCH OF THE EUROPEAN
      WAR: THE SECOND PHASE. Thomas
      Nelson and Sons.
1916 THE SECOND YEAR OF THE WAR.
      Reprinted by permission from Land and
      Water: Burrup, Mathieson and Sprague.
1918 THE FREE PRESS. George Allen and
      Unwin.
1918 RELIGION AND CIVIL LIBERTY. Catholic
      Truth Society.
1919 THE PRINCIPLES OF WAR, by Marshal
      Foch. Translated by Hilaire Belloc.
      Chapman and Hall.
1919 PRECEPTS AND JUDGMENTS, by Marshal
      Foch. Translated by Hilaire Belloc.
      Chapman and Hall.

1920 THE CATHOLIC CHURCH AND THE PRINCIPLE OF PRIVATE PROPERTY. Catholic Truth Society.

1920 EUROPE AND THE FAITH. Constable and Co.

1920 THE HOUSE OF COMMONS AND MONARCHY. George Allen and Unwin.

1921 PASCAL'S 'PROVINCIAL LETTERS'. Catholic Truth Society.

1922 CATHOLIC SOCIAL REFORM VERSUS SOCIALISM. Catholic Truth Society.

1922 THE JEWS. Constable and Co.

1922 THE MERCY OF ALLAH. Chatto and Windus.

1923 ON. Methuen and Co.

1923 THE ROAD. Manchester: Charles W. Hobson.

1923 SONNETS AND VERSE. Duckworth and Co.

1923 THE CONTRAST. J. W. Arrowsmith (London) Ltd.

1924 ECONOMICS FOR HELEN. J. W. Arrowsmith (London) Ltd.

1924 THE CAMPAIGN OF 1812. Thomas Nelson and Sons.

1924 THE POLITICAL EFFORT. True Temperance Association.

1925 THE CRUISE OF THE 'NONA'. Constable and Co.

1925 A HISTORY OF ENGLAND: Vol. I. Methuen and Co.

1925 MR. PETRE. Arrowsmith.

1925 MINIATURES OF FRENCH HISTORY. Thomas Nelson and Sons.

1925 ENGLAND AND THE FAITH. A Reply published in the Evening Standard to an article by Dean Inge in the same journal. Catholic Truth Society.

1926 THE HIGHWAY AND ITS VEHICLES. The Studio Ltd.

1926 SHORT TALKS WITH THE DEAD. The Cayme Press.

1926 MRS. MARKHAM'S NEW HISTORY OF ENGLAND. The Cayme Press.

1926 THE EMERALD. Arrowsmith.

1926 A COMPANION TO MR. WELTS'S 'OUTLINE OF HISTORY'. Sheed and Ward.

1926 MR. BELLOC STILL OBJECTS. Sheed and Ward.

1927 THE CATHOLIC CHURCH AND HISTORY. Burns Oates and Washbourne.

1927 A HISTORY OF ENGLAND: Vol II. Methuen and Co.

1927 THE HAUNTED HOUSE. Arrowsmith.

1927 OLIVER CROMWELL. Ernest Berm.

1928 MANY CITIES. Constable and Co.

1928 A HISTORY OF ENGLAND: Vol. III. Methuen and Co.

1928 JAMES THE SECOND. Faber and Gwyer.

1928 HOW THE REFORMATION HAPPENED. Jonathan Cape.

1928 BUT SOFT – WE ARE OBSERVED. Arrowsmith.

1928 A CONVERSATION WITH AN ANGEL. Jonathan Cape.

1928 BELINDA. Constable and Co.

1929 SURVIVALS AND NEW ARRIVALS. Sheed and Ward.

1929 JOAN OF ARC. Cassell and Co.

1929 THE MISSING MASTERPIECE. Arrowsmith.

1930 RLCHELIEU. Ernest Benn.

1930 A PAMPHLET. (Privately printed for H.B.'s sixtiethlbirthday.)

1930 WOLSEY. Cassell and Co.

1930 THE MAN WHO MADE GOLD. Arrowsmith.

1930 NEW CAUTIONARY TALES. Duckworth.

1931 A CONVERSATION WITH A CAT. Cassell and Co.

1931 ON TRANSLATION. (The Taylorian Lecture). Oxford: The Clarendon Press.

1931 ESSAYS OF A CATHOLIC. Sheed and Ward

1931 A HISTORY OF ENGLAND: Vol. IV. Methuen and Co.

1931 CRANMER. Cassell and Co.

193 1 TRAVEL NOTES ON A HOLIDAY TOUR IN FRANCE, by James Murray Allison, with an introduction and commentary by Hilaire Belloc. Privately printed.

1931 THE PRAISE OF WINE. AN HEROIC POEM to Duff Cooper. (1) No imprint. Presented by H.B. to his friends for Christmas . IQ3I. (2) An Heroic Poem ill Praise of Wine. Peter Davies (1932.)

1932 THE POSTMASTER-GENERAL. Arrowsmith.

1932 LADIES AND GENTLEMEN. Duckworth.

1932 NAPOLEON. Cassell and Co.

1933   THE TACTICS AND STRATEGY OF THE GREAT DUKE OF MARLBOROUGH. Arrowsmith.

1933   WILLIAM THE CONQUEROR. Peter Davies.

1933   BECKET. Catholic Truth Society. (Published also by Sheed and Ward (1933) in 'The English Way', a collection of essays by various authors.)

1933   CHARLES THE FIRST. Cassell and Co.

1934   CROMWELL. Cassell and Co.

1934   A SHORTER HISTORY OF ENGLAND. George G. Harrap and Co.

1935   MILTON. Cassell and Co.

1936   THE BATTLE GROUND. Cassell and Co.

1936   THE COUNTY OF SUSSEX. Cassell and Co.

1936   AN ESSAY ON THE RESTORATION OF PROPERTY. The Distributist League.

1936   CHARACTERS OF THE REFORMATION. Sheed ifud Ward.

1936   THE HEDGE AND THE HORSE. Cassell and Co.

1937   AN ESSAY ON THE NATURE OF CONTEMPORARY ENGLAND. Constable and Co.

1937   THE CRUSADE. Cassell and Co.

1937   THE CRISIS OF OUR CIVILIZATION. Cassell and Co.

1938   SONNETS AND VERSE. Duckworth. New edition, with additional poems.

1938   THE GREAT HERESIES. Sheed and Ward.

1938   RETURN TO THE BALTIC. Constable and Co.

193 8   THE QUESTION AND THE ANSWER. Longmans, Green and Co.

1938   MONARCHY: A Study of Louis XIV. Cassell and Co.

1938   THE CASE OF DR. COULTON. Sheed and Ward.

1939   ON SAILING THE SEA. Methuen and Co.

1940   THE LAST RALLY. Cassell and Co.

1940   THE CATHOLIC AND THE WAR. Burns Oates.

1940   ON THE PLACE OF GILBERT CHESTERTON IN ENGLISH LETTERS,. Sheed and Ward.

1941   THE SILENCE OF THE SEA. Cassell and Co.

1942   ELIZABETHAN COMMENTARY. Cassell and Co.

1942   PLACES. Cassell and Co.

1954   THE VERSE OF HILAIRE BELLOC. The Nonesuch Press.

1955   ONE THING AND ANOTHER. Hollis and Carter.

Acknowledgements

The author is especially indebted to his three proof-readers: Oskar Shorts, Paul Deacon, and Caroline Ransom, without whom this book would certainly be littered with an excess of commas! Their suggestions and encouragement were much appreciated.

Simon and Mike Blacker at Blacker Design have worked tirelessly to ensure the book is both readable and attractive.

Thanks to my wife, Ann Feloy, for her support and helpful comments regarding the introduction and the cover, and for doing a final proof-read of the entire text.

Thanks also to Peter and Jenny Bennett who suggested I should write this book as a series of themed chapters: had I not taken this advice I might still be writing now and writing far too much.

I am grateful to West Sussex Record Office for their permission to reproduce the photographs of Belloc and his family in their possession, and the photographs from the Garland Collection. Thanks to Sussex Archaeological Society for permission to reproduce the 1885 photograph of Devil's Dyke and the photograph of the ploughing team.

The publication of this book was made possible by a grant from the National Lottery Heritage Fund, as part of the Belloc, Broadwood and Beyond project, www.belloc-broadwood.org.uk. Information about the Hilaire Belloc Society can be found at the hilairebellocblog.blogspot.com

Index